# Sándor Ferenc

This book aims to present an up-to-date introduction and critical study of one of the most important psychoanalysts of all time, Sándor Ferenczi.

The book presents Ferenczi as a person; his discovery of psychoanalysis and his relationship with Freud; the theoretical and clinical novelties he introduced to psychoanalysis; his deep political and social commitment, striving for the democratization of psychoanalysis; and the great relevance of his thought and perspective for the future. It also talks about his repression in the history of psychoanalysis as well as his influence in the following generations of psychoanalysts. The reader will be presented with the most relevant historical milestones and concepts, with new insights regarding some of Ferenczi's most fundamental ideas (such as his trauma theory, his technical innovations or his developments regarding the end of analysis), as well as an informed viewpoint of his legacy, the contemporary readings of his work and the institutions and associations that continue following the path traced by l'enfant terrible of psychoanalysis.

This book will be of interest both for the novel reader who has had none or scarce contact with the person and/or work of Sándor Ferenczi, as well as to the psychoanalysts, clinicians and scholars, who have a deeper contact and understanding of the work of the Hungarian analyst.

**Alberto Fergusson, M.D.** is a psychiatrist and psychoanalyst working in Colombia and in the United States. Since 1982, he has been the head and founder of the Institute of Accompanied Self-Rehabilitation. He was also the Founder of FUNGRATA in Colombia and FAS in Washington DC. He is currently Director and Full Professor at the Center for Psychosocial Studies (CEPPS) of the Universidad del Rosario, Colombia. He has been actively involved in the peace process in Colombia, at present as advisor to the president of the Truth Commission.

**Miguel Gutiérrez-Peláez, Ph.D.,** is a Full Professor at the Center for Psychosocial Studies (CEPSS) of the Universidad del Rosario, Colombia and has been part of the Psychology Program since 2011. He is a member of the World Association of Psychoanalysis (AMP) and the New Lacanian School (NEL) and has his clinical practice in Colombia. He is author of the book *Confusion of Tongues: A Return to Sándor Ferenczi* (Routledge, 2018).

# Routledge Introductions to Contemporary Psychoanalysis

**Aner Govrin**
Series Editor
**Tair Caspi**
Associate Editor

Books in the Routledge Introductions to Contemporary Psychoanalysis will serve as concise introductions dedicated to influential concepts, theories, leading figures, and techniques in psychoanalysis.

The length of each book is fixed at 40,000 words.

The series' books are designed to be easily accessible so as to provide informative answers in various areas of psychoanalytic thought. Each book will provide updated ideas on topics relevant to contemporary psychoanalysis – from the unconscious and dreams, projective identification and eating disorders, through neuropsychoanalysis, colonialism and spiritual-sensitive psychoanalysis. Books will also be dedicated to prominent figures in the field, such as Melanie Klein, Jaque Lacan, Sandor Ferenczi, Otto Kernberg and Michael Eigen.

Not serving solely as an introduction for beginners, the purpose of the series is to offer compendiums of information on particular topics within different psychoanalytic schools. We ask authors to review a topic but also address the readers with their own personal views and contribution to the specific chosen field. Books will make intricate ideas comprehensible without compromising their complexity.

We aim to make contemporary psychoanalysis more accessible to both clinicians and the general educated public.

**Published Titles**

Projective Identification: A Contemporary Introduction
*By Robert Waska*

Donald Meltzer: A Contemporary Introduction
*By Meg Harris Williams*

Sándor Ferenczi: A Contemporary Introduction
*By Alberto Fergusson & Miguel Gutiérrez-Peláez*

# Sándor Ferenczi

## A Contemporary Introduction

## Alberto Fergusson and Miguel Gutiérrez-Peláez

Routledge
Taylor & Francis Group

LONDON AND NEW YORK

First published 2022
by Routledge
2 Park Square, Milton Park, Abingdon, Oxon OX14 4RN

and by Routledge
605 Third Avenue, New York, NY 10158

*Routledge is an imprint of the Taylor & Francis Group, an informa business*

© 2022 Alberto Fergusson and Miguel Gutiérrez-Peláez

*British Library Cataloguing-in-Publication Data*
A catalogue record for this book is available from the British Library

*Library of Congress Cataloging-in-Publication Data*
Names: Fergusson, Alberto, author. | Gutiérrez-Peláez, Miguel, author.
Title: Sándor Ferenczi : a contemporary introduction / Alberto Fergusson & Miguel Gutiérrez-Peláez.
Description: Abingdon, Oxon ; New York, NY : Routledge, 2022. | Series: Routledge introductions to contemporary psychoanalysis | Includes bibliographical references and index. |
Identifiers: LCCN 2021040710 (print) | LCCN 2021040711 (ebook) | ISBN 9780367426750 (hardback) | ISBN 9780367426767 (paperback) | ISBN 9780367854355 (ebook)
Subjects: LCSH: Ferenczi, Sándor, 1873-1933. | Psychoanalysts. | Psychoanalysis.
Classification: LCC RC339.52.F48 F47 2022 (print) | LCC RC339.52.F48 (ebook) | DDC 616.89/17--dc23
LC record available at https://lccn.loc.gov/2021040710
LC ebook record available at https://lccn.loc.gov/2021040711

ISBN: 978-0-367-42675-0 (hbk)
ISBN: 978-0-367-42676-7 (pbk)
ISBN: 978-0-367-85435-5 (ebk)

DOI: 10.4324/9780367854355

Typeset in Times New Roman
by MPS Limited, Dehradun

Alberto Fergusson:

To my four children and six grandchildren.

Miguel Gutiérrez-Peláez:

To my sons for teaching me about things no book can teach.

# Contents

*Acknowledgements*                                              xi

Introduction                                                     1

1 The democratisation of psychoanalysis.
  Sándor Ferenczi, from forced disappearance
  to resurrection                                                4

2 Sándor Ferenczi's biographical outline                        9

3 Ferenczi's encounter with psychoanalysis                     15

4 Ferenczi as a translator and divulgater of
  Freud's work                                                  27

5 The concept of "Introjection"                                31

6 Ferenczi's introduction of technical innovations             40

7 Thalassa and bioanalysis                                     57

8 The end of analysis                                          60

 9 Ferenczi's interest in the psychology of the
   child: upbringing and education                        68

10 Ferenczi's latest writings. The effect of
   "confusion of tongues" and his *Clinical Diary*        72

11 Ferenczi's trauma theory                               81

12 Splitting as a psychic defence                         87

13 The repression of Ferenczi's work and the
   return of the repressed                               100

14 Ferenczi's legacy and place in the world today        107

15 What is the relevance of Ferenczi in the
   future?                                               112

   *Epilogue*                                            114
   *References*                                          117
   *Index*                                               122

# Acknowledgements

Alberto Fergusson would like to thank:

All the people that have shared their inner life with me where we have all benefited from mutual analysis.

Miguel Gutiérrez-Peláez would like to thank:

Aner Govrin and Tair Caspi for their invitation to write this book on Sándor Ferenczi for the *Routledge Psychoanalytic Introductions*. Susannah Frearson for her aid and logistical assistance. Judit Mészáros for her generosity, support and key contributions. Laura Natalia Salgado, Henry Mateo Garay, Juan Kamilo Ricci, Isabella Quiroz, Maria Fernanda Bustos, Andrés Felipe Valbuena and Laura Sofía Daza for their participation as research assistants in the Sándor Ferenczi research project. Great thanks to the CRAI service at the Universidad del Rosario for aiding me in the access to bibliography for this research. To Oliver Müller, profesor at the psychology Program at the Universidad del Rosario for aiding me in a deeper understanding of certain German terms. To Alonso Jiménez for bringing art and fresh insights in times of crisis. To the *Center for Psychosocial Studies* (*CEPSS*) at the Universidad del Rosario, in Bogotá, Colombia for being such a fertile think (and action) tank. To my father, lucid and always willing reader of my work. To my family and friends for enduring my states of Ferenczian passion.

# Introduction

The original title of the first manuscript and the research project
that led to the writing of this book was: "The democratisation of
psychoanalysis Sándor Ferenczi, from forced disappearance to
resurrection". We have used it as the title for Chapter 1 because
it shows right from the start three ideas that are central to both
Sandor Ferenczi and his work. In the first place, he began a
movement that has been struggling ever since, to democratise not
only the practice of psychoanalysis (mutual analysis and other
developments) but also its theory and the way in which psychoanalytic societies operate. Secondly, evidence shows how Ferenczi
and his ideas were forcefully disappeared from the psychoanalytic
movement, for example, by censoring and actively removing his
writings from publication and dissemination. Thirdly, thanks to
the fact that some people including but not limited to analysts
took action, the person and his work somehow resurrected.
They are gradually finding the right place in the history of psychoanalysis and of the ground-breaking thinkers and clinicians
of the XX century. Our book hopefully is part of this process of
resurrection.

This book aims to present an up-to-date introduction and critical
study of one of the most important psychoanalysts of all times, who
came to be known as Sigmund Freud's most brilliant pupil: Sándor
Ferenczi. Of him, Freud said: "Hungary, so close to Austria geo-
graphically and so distanced scientifically, up to now has offered
psychoanalysis only one collaborator, S. Ferenczi; but such a one

DOI: 10.4324/9780367854355-101

that he is worth an entire society". This introduction presents Ferenczi as a person; his discovery of psychoanalysis and his relationship with Freud; the theoretical and clinical novelties he introduced to psychoanalysis; his unique contributions to the comprehension and treatment of psychological trauma; his distance with Freud and his repression in the history of psychoanalysis; his influence in the following generations of psychoanalysts even though many did not cite him; his return to the psychoanalytic scene; his influence in psychoanalysis today; and the great relevance of his thought and perspective for the future.

Ferenczi was a leftist intellectual, devoted to social change and politically active. His polemic clinical innovations can be understood as deeply revolutionary, inserting radical democratization of the psychoanalytic setting. In a sense, his technical innovation of "mutual analysis", undoubtedly the most radical one, is, a subversion of the hierarchical functioning of the doctor-patient relationship. Ferenczi believed psychoanalysis was a vehicle for social and political transformation. The patients, as the oppressed and stigmatised sectors of society, were able to gain liberty through psychoanalysis, becoming aware of the social and psychical forces that condition them and being able to grasp within them a true and authentic self.

This book is of interest both for the novel reader who has had none or scarce contact with the person and/or work of Sándor Ferenczi, as well as to the psychoanalysts, clinicians and scholars, who have a deeper contact and understanding of the work of the Hungarian analyst. The reader will be led through the life and work of Ferenczi, presenting the most relevant historical milestones and concepts, with new insights regarding some of his most fundamental ideas (such as his trauma theory, his technical innovations or his developments regarding the end of analysis), as well as an informed viewpoint of his legacy, the contemporary readings of his work and the institutions and associations that continue following the path traced by *l'enfant terrible* of psychoanalysis. We believe the reader will be able to grasp in depth the transcendence of Ferenczi's ideas and the vitality of his clinical and theoretical work, which can offer a clearing for psychoanalysis in our current times and our future.

The ideas presented in this book are a product of the dialogue and analysis of both authors, discussed extensively throughout the years of academic, intellectual and practical activities at the *Center for Psychosocial Studies* (CEPSS), to a point that it is not possible to distinguish which ideas belong to each. The original draft of the book was written by Miguel Gutiérrez-Peláez, except Chapter 1, which was written by Alberto Fergusson. The conceptualisation, review and editing of the final draft were carried out by both authors.

Chapter 1

# The democratisation of psychoanalysis. Sándor Ferenczi, from forced disappearance to resurrection

Throughout history, we find several examples of great thinkers who have been buried alive. This was especially true during the 20th century and amongst them, Sigmund Freud and Karl Marx constitute the most outstanding examples of that very peculiar phenomenon. We are talking, of course, of thinkers whose ideas are officially considered not valid without ever been really disproven. Sometimes, like in the case of Freud and Marx, those ideas together with their authors are buried alive, but not disappeared. Clear example of that is how the great Frankfurt school brought to light not only the two individuals, but also the intrinsic links between the two. Everybody talks about them, mainly against them, frequently without having read them. They were certainly not disappeared. In other cases, people and their ideas are not just buried alive. They are also subject to forced disappearance. Sándor Ferenczi was a clear example of that, until he had a forced resurrection mainly due to the publication of his *Clinical Diary* (1932) and to all that we learned through the analysis of Elizabeth Severn. It is worthwhile to remember some details about the way that Ferenczi's ideas disappeared in so far as it shows a procedure that has been used again and again in psychoanalytic societies belonging to the most diverse schools of thought.

It seems that Freud and other analysts played an active role in omitting the publication in English of Ferenczi's paper "Confusion of tongues between the adult and the child" (1932)

DOI: 10.4324/9780367854355-1

(see Rachman, 1989). Ernest Jones told Ferenczi that he had translated the paper and that it would be published in the following volume of the *International Journal of Psychoanalysis*. After Ferenczi's death in May 1933, Jones wrote to Freud telling him that he was against the publishing of the paper:

> Since [Ferenczi's] death, I have been thinking over the removal of the personal reasons for publishing it. Others also have suggested that it now be withdrawn and I quote the following passage from a letter of Mrs. Riviere's with which I agree: 'Now that Ferenczi has died, I wondered whether you will not reconsider publishing his last paper. It seems to me it can only be damaging to him and a discredit, while now that he is no longer to be hurt by its not being published, no good purpose could be served by it. Its scientific contentions and its statements about analytic practice are just a tissue of delusions, which can only discredit psychoanalysis and give credit to its opponents. It cannot be supposed that all Journal readers will appreciate the mental condition of the writer, and in this respect, one has to think of posterity, too!' I therefore think it best to withdraw the paper unless I hear from you that you have any wish to the contrary " (unpublished letter, Jones Archives, London, cited in Masson, p. 152; Rachman, 1989, p. 199, Gutiérrez-Peláez, 2018.)

There is no evidence of Freud's response to Jones' and Riverie's petition, but the truth is that the paper was not published. It will be until 1949, 16 years later that a version of the paper in English, translated by Michael Balint, will be finally made public. Those who have been disappeared and/or buried alive are typically people that up to a certain point have been slightly ahead of their own time. We emphasise slightly, because they usually say things that are about to be said by others. They are let's say preconscious, to use Freud's language or the objective conditions for them to flourish are there, if we prefer to use the language of historical materialism. We find that ideas that have been buried alive and disappeared are many years later published by another analyst, frequently without quoting the initial one. It can be accepted that this can happen because of real ignorance, due precisely to the fact that they were in fact disappeared. Not every disappeared analyst has the luck Ferenczi had in being subjected to a process of resurrection. Many will probably remain disappeared forever like it happens in most wars. A colleague of ours, who read the manuscript of this book, said that our affirmation of disappearance would also be subject to a similar process of disappearance. We hope not, and if you are reading this right now, it certainly means that this did not happened.

Amongst other reasons, what we have just described led us to develop the concept of a "Viennese Psychoanalysis" to describe not only Freud's ideas, but the developments that happened during the early stages of psychoanalysis, including the first and second generation. Most of those contributions were certainly also buried alive and some were disappeared as we have stated. Ferenczi is an outstanding representative of that group, but certainly not the only one. The attitude, the energy, the connection with the real world that Viennese psychoanalysis had, which in fact did spread throughout other countries in the region, was later repressed in what Jacoby called the repression of psychoanalysis, especially when that repression created so called "orthodox psychoanalysis", which was certainly not Freudian analysis as it was clearly shown by Beate Losher and Peter M. Newton (1996) in *Unorthodox Freud*. The revolution of psychoanalysis included not only a very active participation in politics and progressive social movements, but it changed forever all the human sciences including art and philosophy, and sociology, as it was nicely pointed out by Carlos Alberto Castillo Mendoza (2005). The importance that Ferenczi gave to the relation between psychology and the social was very deep. Adorno had already stated that Ferenczi was the most firm and free spirit within the psychoanalytic movement (Adorno, 1986, quoted by Castillo Mendoza, 2005, p. 56). Sociology had to rethink itself after Ferenczi. Partial disappearance of the ideas and emery of some psychoanalysts happened following similar dynamics in particular when they were forced to "behave properly" especially from a political point of view. This was, of course, dramatically increased once many of them had to fly into exile due to Nazi persecution. The case of Otto Fenichel, beautifully described by Russell Jacoby (1983), was of the most the typical examples.

Ferenczi began what we would like to call a process of democratisation of psychoanalysis in its theory, its technique and, up to a certain point, in the way Institutes and Societies function in psychoanalytic societies. His acceptance of mutual analysis is a much wider and I would like to say revolutionary concept, than what it has generally been accepted. Mutual analysis is present in every psychoanalytic process. Every analysand does it although it is done in a somewhat unconscious and covered manner. Frequently they use basically the same analytic technique that the analyst is using. What happened with Elizabeth Severn and Ferenczi is just a more explicit and open way to something that up to a certain way always happens in a somewhat clandestine way between them and later it became public. While writing this book, we became conscious of the way through which we have practiced mutual analysis in every analysis. Through our work with Accompanied auto analysis (later called accompanied self-rehabilitation) (Fergusson, 2015b), we practiced mutual analysis consciously in most instances. We came to think that this was something we did only while working with so-called homeless mentally ill people. We now acknowledge that we do it all the time in a not so explicit way. It is only through explicit mutual analysis or through Accompanied Auto analysis (self-rehabilitation) that the psychoanalysis can overcome its hierarchical and authoritarian attitude in theory, in practice and, as we pointed out, in the way our Societies function. On the other hand, it has been recognised by others that one of the earliest experiences in mutual analysis was that of Jung and Otto gross in 1908. Mutual analysis, and its implicit democratisation, implies that the idea that the analyst is the healthy person and the analysand is ill becomes irrelevant to the process and is easy to overcome. As analysts, we owe our gratitude to our analysands who are also inevitably also our analysts. All of us as analysands know perfectly well how we analysed our analysts, but that was never acknowledged. Ferenczi had the courage to be honest and call things by their name. He opened the door to the analysts to do the same thing.

Both the external and the internal world of Ferenczi was full of innovation and creativity. The fact that Ferenczi was the first university professor to be elected democratically says many things about those who elected him but also about him. But even more significant is the fact that in general analysts trained in different psychoanalytic institutes connected with the *International Psychoanalytic Association* (IPA) never really studied Ferenczi in depth, at least not as part of the official curriculum of their institutes. As we know, Ferenczi played a crucial role in organising the IPA.

This book is a way to pay tribute to Ferenczi. Many of us, who have shared his views and, most important of all, his attitude, have found in Sandor Ferenczi's life and work great examples that gives us the strength to carry on in a struggle that by its nature has to be a rather lonely one.

# Chapter 2

# Sándor Ferenczi's biographical outline

As an outstanding mind of the 20th century, Sándor Ferenczi condenses the passion for clinical practice, for the limits and potentiality of the human psyche, for psychoanalysis, the unconscious and madness. He was Freud's most exceptional disciple.

Sándor's father, Bernath Fränkel, was born in Krakov, Poland, and arrived at Hungary as a teenager. It seems he emigrated escaping from the anti-Semitic pogroms in Europe (Johnson, 2004, p. 436). Bernath was part of the patriotic forces who fought against the extension of the Habsburg Empire in Hungary: the failed Hungarian Revolution and the 1848–1849 independence war. This insurrection was swiftly appeased; nonetheless, Bernath remained in Hungary, settling in Miskolcz. Sándor's mother was Rösa Eibenschütz. She was also Polish, but grew up in Vienna.

Bernath obtained a job in a local bookstore owned by an American immigrant named Michael Heilprin. Located in the centre of the city, it specialised in the publication and divulgation of patriotic and radical literature (Stanton, 1997, p. 6). Afterwards, in 1856, Bernath bought the library, making it the family business.

The position of the Jews in Hungary changed during that time and their role was key both in the development of the country, as well as in the development of psychology and the intelligentsia of the end of the nineteenth century and the beginning of the twentieth.

DOI: 10.4324/9780367854355-2

In 1867, an emancipation bill granted equal civil rights to Hungarian Jews. The modernization of the economy needed the Jewish entrepreneurial spirit and soon their contribution to economic growth, as well as to art, science, and culture rose to unparalleled levels. Assimilation, secularization and conversion to Christianity became prominent trends among Hungarian Jews. Wealthy Jewish industrialists received titles of nobility from the Emperor-King Francis Joseph I. In this 'golden age' of the Hungarian Jewry (Patai, 1996) Budapest became a significant centre for Jewish culture. While anti-Semitism was an ever-present current, the Jewish population was assimilated and secularized beyond the European average (Nye, 2011) (…) [N]or modern Hungarian history and culture, nor the history of Hungarian psychology can be understood without understanding the significant role played by Jewish-Hungarians. (Szokolszky, 2016, p. 20)

Sándor was born on July 7, 1873, in Miskolcs (North of Hungary), into the intellectual ambiance of the library, which had grown up to become a place of cultural reference, being a meeting point for intellectual conversations and also small musical concerts. German was the official language of the Habsburg Empire, but a few years before Sándor was born, Hungary adopted the Hungarian as the official language. This led to a change in the writing of the family name from Fränkel to Ferenczi. Sándor was the eighth son of a total of twelve. When he was born, the family was composed by Enric, the oldest brother, Max, Sigmund (allegedly Sándor's favourite brother), Ilona, Maria, Joseph and Gizella. After Sándor, his siblings were Martiz-Caroline, Vilma (who died when Sándor was 8 years old), Lajos and Sofia.

Bernath died at the age of 58, when Sándor was 15 years old. His mother, Rósa, devoted most of her energy to the family business, and Sándor regretted not having had the attention from her that he wished. Little is known of Rósa, besides being the head of a numerous family and actively participating in the union of Jewish women of the city. After Bernath's death, she took active control of the library and of the family finances. She opened a second library in the nearby city of Nyiregyhaza. Ferenczi mentions in his correspondence, for example, in his letters with Groddeck that his mother was severe and that he received from her very little love (Ferenczi/Groddeck, 1921).

When he was 21, Sándor studied medicine, having great interest for both neurology and psychiatry, and received his M.D. from the University of Vienna in 1894, at the age of 21. He was quickly fascinated by the studies on hypnosis and hysteria, which he read about from French medical literature. He later enroled in military service in the Austro-Hungarian army and, later, continued his studies in neurology and psychiatry. As a young adolescent, Ferenczi had an interest in writing poetry, influenced by the German poet Heinrich Heine (1797–1856), and had begun to experiment with hypnosis as a high school student in Miscolcz. In his correspondence and in his *Clinical Diary*, Ferenczi mentioned sexual abuses and excesses he was subjected to: by a nanny who allowed his to caress her breasts and who later pressed his head between her legs, leading him to feel the fear of suffocation, and an event when he was 5 years old when a child a year older than him introduced his penis in Sándor's mouth.

His first job as a doctor was with patients with sexually transmitted diseases in the Rókus Hospital and in the Elizabeth hospital for the poor, granting medical service to the less-favoured population and to prostitutes. In 1899, when he was 26 years old, he published the first of many articles in the *Gyógyàszat* ("Therapy") journal, article that he entitled "*Spiritismus*" and which shows how, from very early, Ferenczi took risks in his writing and displayed creative ideas. *Gyógyàszat* was edited by Miksa Schäcter, which was one the first important intellectual figures for Ferenczi. His interest in these first years of academic publishing revolved around human sexuality, the understanding of hysteria, love, sexual perversions, dreams, homosexuality, unconscious processes, the relation between the body and the mind and the evolution of the human psyche (Erös, 2004, p. 126). It is in this period that he reinforced his interest and study in the French literature on hypnosis and was probably the moment he first came in contact with Freud's work, though he seems to have read it superficially at that time. Schäcter asked Ferenczi to write a commentary of Freud's book, *The interpretation of dreams* (1900), for the journal. Ferenczi read the work and concluded that it was not a book worth taking seriously. This will change dramatically after his acquaintance with Gustav Jung, and later Freud himself, which we will describe later.

During most of his professional life, and before he married Gizella, Ferenczi lived in the *Royal Hotel* in Budapest. The hotel's coffee shop became an important location for intellectual gatherings. Prominent representatives of the Hungarian intelligentsia, such as the poets and writers Dezső Kosztolányi and Sándor Márai (Mészáros, 2010, p. 69), the journalist and writer Frigyes Karinthy, the painter Róbert Berény (member of the "Group of the Eight"), psychoanalyst Lajos Levy, entrepreneur and philanthropist Antal Freund Tószeghi (known as Anton von Freund), neurologist and psychoanalyst Imre Hermann, musician and composer Béla Bártok, philosopher György Lukács, anthropologist Géza Róheim (Jiménez Avello, 1998, p. 44), Karl Mannheim, and art historian Arnold Hauser, as well as members of the "Galileo Group," the "20th Century Group" and the "Radical Intellectuals," amongst other, were frequent participants in the gatherings at the café.

As stated by Szokolszky (2016)

> Ferenczi was also involved in radical socialist circles, as a devotee of social change. At the turn of the century intellectuals hotly debated ways of modernization and fighting backwardness. Young sociologists and politicians led by Oszkár Jászi believed in positivist science and were in favour of radical social reforms, including land ownership [...]. Representatives of this intellectual tapestry not only were decisive in culture, but many of them entered politics during the short-lived revolutionary governments after the First World War. (p. 25)

It was this interest of psychoanalysis in the social sphere and its effect outside the clinic that led to the projects of the free policlinics in Europe. The first one was founded in Berlin and was inaugurated in 1920 (Danto, 2005). The second policlinic, founded in Budapest, had to wait until 1931 to finally function.

The clinics offered free psychoanalytic therapy to people who could not afford it. They were also places for psychoanalytic training, conferences, meetings and group interventions, and arouse great interest among the lay public.

The intellectual discussions around psychoanalysis, which was gaining interest as a new science, summoned not only doctors, but also all kinds of intellectuals, with diverse backgrounds and interests, which ranged from artists, writers, musicians, and critics, and included members of important intellectual groups of that time. Ferenczi's presence in the discussions was key, and it seems he did not compromise his thought in favour of the complacency of others. Regarding the political possibilities of psychoanalysis, Ferenczi mentions on a letter to Freud:

> Once society has gone beyond the infantile, then hitherto completely unimagined possibilities for social and political life are opened up. Just think what it would mean if one *could tell everyone the truth,* one's father, teacher, neighbour, and even the king. All fabricated, imposed authority would go to the devil-what is *rightful* would remain natural. The eradication of lies from private and public life would necessarily have to bring about better conditions" (Brabant, Falzeder, & Giampieri-Deutsch, 1993, p. 130).

His radical, innovative and unorthodox ideas led to awakening others to his original reading and understanding of psychoanalysis. As cited by Erös (2018), Ferenczi stated that

> Psychoanalysis rather joins to Durkheim and not to the Marxist sociology and politics, and, in concrete and actual questions joins to liberal socialism. [...] Psychoanalysis and liberal socialism share the same worldview, the same ethical sense, and the same task in the service of the welfare of men.

Psychoanalysis cannot bring "salvation," but only works "for the self-salvation of the individual."

Ferenczi's insistence on the training of the analyst, on taking the analysis of the analyst to the end, on introducing changes to the analytic technique to favour the patient's needs, led to shake up the psychoanalytic establishment of the time, especially those who wished to make of the psychoanalytic doctrine and technique a set of immobile conventions for the "correct" course of the psychoanalytic cure. As we will see in the following chapters, this was one of the reasons that led to Ferenczi's exclusion from the psychoanalytic scene for decades, until his revival in the sixties and seventies, revival which continues up to now, placing Ferenczi as one of the most original psycho-analyst whose writings and questions raised in the psychoanalytic movement continue to be pertinent and are fundamental for the future perspectives of the discipline.

Chapter 3

# Ferenczi's encounter with psychoanalysis

Sándor Ferenczi was referred to as the *"enfant terrible"* of psychoanalysis. As he mentions in his 1931 paper "Child-Analysis in the Analysis of Adults": "I am fairly generally regarded as a restless spirit, or, as someone recently said to me at Oxford, the *enfant terrible* of psychoanalysis" (p. 127). He was without doubt one of the furthermost lucid spirits of his time (Gallardo, 1996). Many authors have found in Ferenczi the most devoted clinician of the first generation of psychoanalysts and, despite the polemics that surrounded him, he has been thought of as an outstanding therapist. He was prone to receive the most severe and challenging patients, which made him also known as an expert in difficult cases.

Ferenczi was what we could call a leftist liberal, fighting even within the psychoanalytic movement for the defence of homosexuals, population that had been marginalized and persecuted in Europe. He had great interest in the understanding of the psychological functioning of homosexuals, and this led him to be one of the first to link homosexuality with paranoia. As a doctor, Ferenczi was a representative in the International Humanitarian Committee for the Defence of Homosexuals, founded by Magnus Hirschfeld in 1897, fighting for legal reforms and sensitizing the general public in a trend against mainstream psychiatry, that of Richard von Krafft-Ebing and Paul Julius Möbius, who thought of homosexuality as a degenerative disease. Ferenczi was quite critical of his fellow doctors who he found hypocritical in

DOI: 10.4324/9780367854355-3

their ethical standards, which obliged them to fight indistinctly for the welfare of all human beings.

Even as founder and ex-president of the *International Psychoanalytic Association* (*IPA*), he believed in the flexibility of the training of the analyst and the importance of the active technique, and not neutrality, within analysts, for he believed that behind this neutrality laid the analyst's aggression and sadistic hostility. He was also an active defender of the training of non-physicians as psychoanalysts, idea which Freud also supported, as made explicit in his essay "The Question of Lay Analysis" (1926).

## Ferenczi meets Freud

It was via Carl Gustav Jung that Ferenczi became interested in Freud's work. Ferenczi was attracted to Jung's "Word Association Test" and started applying it and making his own measurements. Thanks to the influence of his friend Füllöp Stein (1867–1918), Ferenczi read a series of French works he had passed over before, mainly Breuer and Freud's work on hysteria.

Freud and Ferenczi met for the first time on February 2, 1908. Their first meeting was facilitated by the intervention of Jung and Stein. The latter had worked with Jung since 1906 (Stein will have a brief analysis with Freud, who later will refer him to Ferenczi). Jung had been very interested in Freud's work, which led him to the creation of his "Test," which he had been applying in the Burgholzli clinic of the University of Zurich. These experiments awakened Ferenczi's interest on psychoanalysis.

A series of events lead to Ferenczi and Freud's first meeting. Jung travelled to Vienna on Sunday March 3, 1907 to visit Freud, and attended the Wednesday Meeting of Freud's circle on the afternoon of March 6. The following week, Jung continued to Budapest to meet Stein. Jung and Ferenczi met and had long conversation during this visit. On June 28, Jung wrote to Freud that "Dr. Stein from Budapest and another mental specialist, Dr. Ferenczi, want to visit you for some time in Vienna and have asked me when it would be more convenient for you" (Freud/Jung, June 28, 1907). It was until Sunday, February 2, 1908 (Stanton, 1997, p. 12) that Stein and Ferenczi visited Freud, leading to an acquaintance that will mark a milestone in the development of the psychoanalytic movement. Freud was close to 52 years of age and Ferenczi was 34. Despite the difference of ages, Ferenczi and Freud empathized greatly. Freud invited Ferenczi to present a paper at the First Psychoanalytic Congress in Salzburg and to meet him and his family in Berchtesgaden in August where they spent their summer holidays. A friendship that will last 25 years would thus began.

In his first letters to Freud, Ferenczi wrote about one of his cases, Frau Marton from Tapolcza, and asked for his advice regarding her treatment. According to Ferenczi, Frau Marton suffered from paranoia with delusions of jealousy. This clinical impression was corroborated by Freud, who in turn explained the patient's condition appealing to the separation of the sexual component of the libido which, according to his diagnosis, led her to project herself onto those women of whom she is apparently jealous of, but that in fact is attracted to. Key terms for the evolution of the psychoanalytic theory are constant in their writings, such as paranoia, projection and sublimation, as well as the use of fiction as a therapeutic strategy. They argue that although the case of Frau Marton did not lead to a successful treatment, it allowed advancing in the evidence of psychoanalysis and reaffirming Freud's theories, such as his approach to paranoia, in which "sublimations are destroyed by this projection and the homosexual component in particular comes to the fore" (Brabant et al., 1993, p. 7). Ferenczi stated that "Paranoia is always a case of recrudescent homosexuality" (Braban et al., 1993, p. 22) and Freud flatters Ferenczi's comprehension of the psychic functioning of Frau Marton. In later letters, Freud will continue praising Ferenczi, stating for example that he has made important contributions for his work *Psychopathology of Everyday Life* (1901).

In the second semester of 1908, Ferenczi spent time with Freud during his stay in Berchtesgaden. Concepts such as "the importance of medical transference" were shared in their correspondence. From these first letters, Ferenczi's creativity and novel ideas can be found, such as his conceptualization of "incestuous fixation" as a cause of impotence, and his original thoughts regarding psycho-neurotic's fantasies and the underlying motions in daydreaming. In their letters, they critically discuss the works and ideas of Alfred Adler (his theory of "Inferiority") and of Wilhelm Fliess (his "Periodicity" theory).

In the following months, Ferenczi expressed to Freud his interest in becoming a member of the "Vienna Freud Society," as he named it, and for his application for the society he sent his paper to: "Analytical interpretation and treatment of psychosexual impotence in men." Freud highlighted this paper as worthy of publication and it was eventually published in Johannes Bresler's (1866–1936) journal *Psychiatrisch-neurologische Wochenschrift*).

Ferenczi and Freud planned a trip to Freud's house in Vienna for Christmas 1908. Their relation became each time closer and more familiar. They talked about Freud's children being expectant and excited about seeing Ferenczi once again. Freud will be each time more open with Ferenczi, talking to him about personal matters, such as his anxieties regarding his daughter Matilda's illnesses. They also wrote about their mutual interests, such as Wagner's music and Leonardo da Vinci's art. Their letters are also a place to talk about their everyday anxieties, their achievements and frustrations. For example, in one of them Ferenczi mentions that a fateful month has passed because he lost three patients too soon and now only has two and at "reduced rates," but, despite this, he will give a lecture to the "Local Association of Physicians" about Neurosis and they will pay him 100 crowns. In this lecture, he will seek to discuss treatment methods and their effectiveness. Their correspondence is rich with both quotidian and transcendental events. It is also during this time that Ferenczi gives a lecture on criticism of pre-Freudian therapies and makes a statement on the importance of psychoanalytic therapies.

Freud, Jung and Ferenczi travelled to the US in 1909. Regarding the trip, Freud had said he had no great expectations, except the possibility of traveling with his colleagues and visiting the Niagara Falls. The three men arrived to the US on August 29, spent a week in New York, and then went to Massachusetts, the site of Clark's University. During the following week, Freud delivered his five lectures on psychoanalysis that he planned each morning on his walks with Ferenczi. As Freud (1933) mentioned, "I invited [Ferenczi] to go with me to Worcester, Massachusetts, when in 1909, I was called upon to lecture there during a week of celebrations. In the morning, before the time had come for my lecture to begin, we would walk together in front of the University building and I would ask him to suggest what I should talk about that day. He thereupon gave me a sketch of what, half an hour later, I improvised in my lecture. In this way he had a share in the origin of the *Five Lectures*" (p. 227). Freud and Jung received honorary Doctor of Law degrees during the closing. Afterwards, they visited the Niagara Falls and the James Putnam camp, and left to Bremen on September 29. Jung went home after this, but Freud and Ferenczi stayed a few days in Hamburg and Berlin. At their return, Freud and Ferenczi visited a psychic to investigate Ferenczi's interests in telepathy (Ferenczi will conduct experiments with two psychics: Frau Seidler in Berlin and a few weeks later somnambulist Frau Jelinek) (Rabeyron & Evrard, 2012). Afterwards, the two men wrote extensively regarding this experience.

Their correspondence evidences their each time closer relationship. In *Letter #74*, his first letter after the trip to the United States, Freud refers to Ferenczi as "friend" for the first time. In *Letter 75,* he sends Ferenczi a novel by one of their favourite writers, Anatole France (1844–1924), a novelist and literary critic. Many decades later, Balint (1968) would mention that Ferenczi was the one who maintained the greatest intimacy with Freud of all the analysts of the new generation who gathered around him; he was the first to be called by Freud "dear friend" in his letters, the only one who was invited to travel with him during his most precious vacations. During their lifetime, Freud and Ferenczi passed many vacations together, in Berchtesgaden (1908), USA (1909), Leyden, Paris, Roma, Naples, Palermo and Syracuse (1910), the Dolomites (1911), Roma (1912), Dalmatia (1912) and in Corfu, Greece (1913).

## Ferenczi as Freud's pupil, friend, analysand and colleague

Ferenczi's analysis with Freud was carried out in three different moments: the first, in October 1914 and the second and third between June and October 1916. Each of the three moments lasted approximately nine weeks, carrying out several sessions each day. Ferenczi was Freud's analysand for three weeks in 1914, but had to interrupt his analysis to comply with his military duties in the Hungarian front. He continued his analysis in 1916 for another three weeks, two hours each day.

The second volume of the Freud–Ferenczi correspondence begins before the outbreak of the First World War and ends in the post-war period (1914–1919). Throughout the content of 131 letters, five (5) central topics can be distinguished: the analysis between Freud and Ferenczi, the personal impact of the war, Ferenczi's relationship with Gizella Palos and Elma, her daughter, and the development of techniques and theoretical conceptions within psychoanalysis.

Regarding the development of the techniques and theoretical conceptions, Freud and Ferenczi discussed the issues related to the psychic mechanism of melancholy, which is part of their interest in understanding narcissistic neuroses. In these letters, the idea of an incomprehensible element in mourning appeared repeatedly, which in this case is the difficult issue of the detachment of the libido, which is suffered in a very significant way. Ferenczi then strengthens the understanding of this mechanism by adding the notion of melancholy as something intermediate between transference and narcissistic neurosis as such. He also thinks that melancholy would be, if it is analysed from this point of view, the true introjection psychosis as opposed to hysteria and paranoia. In a later letter, he talks about melancholic suicide, which for him it is a double suicide, since it is both murdering oneself and murdering the ego of his loved one. He also writes how melancholy leads to impoverishment and devaluation of the ego, as well as an overly conscious self-criticism.

Just as part of these novel theoretical insights, Ferenczi mentions his desire to write the book titled *Thalassa*. About this project, which we will discuss in Chapter 6, Ferenczi mentions that he is very interested in approaching the problem of sexual intercourse and to develop his ideas on evolution and sexuality, supported by his readings on contemporary biology. He has been reading texts on embryology, zoology, and comparative physiology, as well as studies on experimental fertilization and is interested in developing a series of essays entitled "Bioanalytic Essays," which would be focused on a meta-psychological and meta-biological analysis of topics such as ontogeny and phylogeny of genitality, sleep, laughter, phylogeny of secondary sexual characteristics and regression and progression in biology.

Ferenczi had a series of somatic symptoms throughout his life, such as chest pains (which he attributed to his "hypochondria"), gastric bleedings, headaches, heartaches, breathing difficulties, severe exhaustion and great concern for his death. This was a matter he worked on in his own analysis, establishing very keen thoughts on the relation between the body and the mind. Ferenczi wrote about somatic experiences which he linked to emotions and repression, such as tics, stammering, creating the basis of future developments on the theory of psychosomatics and somatic psychology. He believed that the body could have a form of non-verbal memory, which produced changes in the body and had effects on the body's adaptation to the external world.

The theme of these phylogenetic approaches as the origin of neuroses appear repeatedly in the correspondence of the two psychoanalysts. Freud says that what are now neuroses were previously phases of the human condition. With the appearance of deprivation during the ice age, humans began to transform their libido into anxiety. Humanity understood that propagation was an activity that had to be restricted to favour its own survival and, in this way, gave rise to the development of hysteria. Obsessive neurosis arose as a defence against the two prohibitions of the original father; later, with his death and the triumph of his children, mania and melancholy arose. Following this line of thought, he suggest that early dementia arose with castration and the renunciation of the sexual object. Ferenczi responds to this letter by relating the advantageous understanding and prevalence of precocious dementia in Northern cultures, which would suggest that Northern men have not yet fully overcome the last period of the ice age. He confesses that he previously associated early dementia with to the hibernation of animals, because he thought that sleep was the most effective type of dementia. Freud concludes the discussion by commenting that he plans to reference

Ferenczi's work on the influence of geological vicissitudes, since he considers them to be original and fruitful ideas. He also adds that he has given him the impetus to develop a longer presentation, which he will share with Ferenczi before publication. In a later letter, Ferenczi returns to the subject and describes the religious phase of humanity with its exaggerated sense of sin, which persists in his time, as the last offspring of melancholy and concludes that psychoanalysis means emancipation of the unjustified authority of religion, as well as the emancipation of exaggerated rebellion against it, which is the beginning of the objective scientific phase. Ferenczi expresses his doubts regarding the analogy with precocious dementia and castration and also mentions that the fixation of homosexuality seems enigmatic to him.

Another topic which is thoroughly worked through in the Freud–Ferenczi correspondence is the conception of detoxification in the treatment of addictions. Ferenczi shares with Freud brief reports of some of the patients he is treating. He mentions one of his patients, a doctor who is addicted to cocaine and is receiving therapy at the same time than detox. Ferenczi had previously tried to analyse this doctor, who was receiving therapy with insurmountable resistance, but this time the resistance gave way to catharsis and to very intense reflections, eventually leading the patient to a state of paranoid dementia. The immediate suspension of therapy and generous doses of cocaine managed to bring him back from that state. During that same period of time, Ferenczi takes one of his friends, First Lieutenant Barthodeiszky, to a sanatorium in Budapest because, after a fight with his commander, he had fallen into a state of manic emotion with homosexual and paranoid characteristics. Barthodeiszky had previously been an alcoholic, leading Ferenczi to believe that there is a latent paranoid predilection for "poisons" (cocaine, alcohol) and that they seem to experience some kind of passive gratification from drug intoxication. Freud responds by stating that intoxication and withdrawal syndrome associated with cocaine lead to a paranoid disease and mentions that he himself witnessed this process in one of his first patients. He believes that the use of therapy to treat intoxications is not very effective for every impulse of resistance is discharged in the relapse.

Within their correspondence, the importance of the analysis in the relationship between the two psychoanalysts can also be highlighted. On September 2, 1914, faced with the imminent possibility of being summoned to enlist in the army, Ferenczi began to use his time in an attempt to carry out a sort of self-analysis, because he believed he did not have enough concentration to carry out any other activity and, in turn, knew that he would not be able to meet with Freud for his psychoanalysis for a long time. Frenczi has his first analytical sessions with Freud in 1914, being this the year when Freud wrote the article "Remarks on transference love," in which the topic of countertransference is again dealt with. As we will see later, this will be one of Ferenczi's main criticisms of his analysis with Freud, as it is made explicit in his correspondence and in his *Clinical Diary* (1932), stating that his analyst has not allowed him to display his negative transference with him.

When he was in Pápa, Hungary, performing his work as a doctor of the Hungarian army, he spend his free time thinking about his self-analysis, fragments of which he incorporated into the letters he sent to Freud. He clarified to Freud that he used the method of free association in his writings to be able to do it in a much freer way. He also talked about the fluctuations in his emotional state, which usually oscillates between apathy and melancholy. Ferenczi remembers sometime later, in January 1916, his stay in Pápa with a certain affection. He thinks that the ideas he had at the time could originate in that environment suitable for isolation, where there was a lack of concern for sustenance and for the future, similar to what occurs in embryonic stages. Ferenczi maintained at the time a somewhat erratic writing style, influenced by free association and by the emotional charge of the topics referred to. Recurring themes that could be highlighted are his guilt and shame for the confession of masturbation and the discomfort caused by the lack of analysis with Freud, where his self-analysis appears as an attempt to replace it. Ferenczi mentions repeatedly the importance of his analysis, admitting in one of his letters that it was one of the most important and significant event of his life.

The impact of war did not deviate Ferenczi from his deep social commitment and political convictions. "During the war he set up an informal psychoanalytic clinic where 'war neurosis' cases, and also people who could not afford paying were treated" (Szokolszky, 2016, p. 24). Also, Ferenczi translated, during his years in Papa, Freud's book "Three essays on the theory of sexuality."

The growing and complex relationship between Ferenczi and Freud is a matter of great interest. The importance that Freud acquires in Ferenczi's life and vice versa can be evidenced. This is quite evident in their correspondence in the frequent mentions to the long stays in which Ferenczi carried out his analysis with him, in the theoretical development in which both contributed innovative and profound ideas to the understanding of psychic functioning, in the fact that both immensely appreciated their advice regarding both personal and editorial decisions, and in the immense confidence they had to speak frankly about the conclusions to which they came in relation to their own mental functioning. Freud sometimes seems to be a father figure to Ferenczi, but also a friend and colleague. This appears to have allowed personal and conceptual feedback and growth for both. Ferenczi says that the arrival of Freud to his life was something that embellished his work and his conception of the world and, on the other hand, Ferenczi was growing in importance for Freud, becoming central figure in his life and professional developments.

The idea of carrying out a self-analysis and revealing his findings to Freud can also be seen as a way of fostering a more personal approach. In a letter sent in December 31, 1914, Ferenczi mentions that in their last meeting he perceived in his own conduct a frankness and a lack of inhibition that is the fruit of the analytical tone with which he wrote some of his letters.

## The Gizella-Elma affair

The relationship between Ferenczi and Gizella Pálos is a key topic of their letters of these years. The beginning of the story can be traced to Ferenczi's childhood and adolescence, for Ferenczi's family was close to the Altschul family. When Sándor was 15 years old, Gizella Altschul, who was by the time 23 years old, married

Géza Pálos, with whom she would have two daughters: Elma and Magda. Magda would eventually marry Lajos, Sándor's younger brother. Gizella will play an important role in Ferenczi's emotional life and will be an important topic of Ferenczi's analysis with Freud. Ferenczi fell deeply in love with Gizella and, later, with her daughter Elma.

When Ferenczi was 31 years old, he began a sentimental relationship with Gizella Palos, 8 years older than him, who was separated from her husband, but not legally divorced because her husband refused to do so. This led to a clandestine relationship between Gizella and Sándor. After seven years of this relationship, Gizella's daughter Elma, now 24, consulted Ferenczi for therapy, for she felt depressed after the suicide of her boyfriend. Elma seems to have been an attractive and emotionally unstable young woman who captivated Ferenczi. Ferenczi wrote to Freud telling him about his feelings towards Elma and how he felt incapable of maintaining his psychoanalytic neutrality. Ferenczi decided to end Elma's treatment and, after some resistance, Freud agreed to continue analysing her.

This Oedipical scenario is quite complex. Gizella was aware of the situation and was willing to step aside if this was in the best interest of her daughter and Ferenczi. Gizella knew she could not have more children and that Ferenczi longed to be a father. From his letters to Ferenczi, we get the impression that this can be one of the scenarios were Freud was not rigorous enough with his own concepts. He seems to be trying to discover if she was in fact in love with Ferenczi of if it was due to transference. It is worth mentioning that Freud wrote "On the dynamics of transference love" and "Advice to the doctor on psychoanalytic treatment" in 1912, the year in which the "Gizella-Elma affair" took place. Freud analysed Elma for three months and later Ferenczi retook the analysis for another five months. It seems that in this second analytical experience, Ferenczi was able to take hold of his feelings and countertransference and separate from Elma both affective and analytically. After her analysis, Elma travelled to the United States and eventually married an American by the last name Laurvick. On his part, Ferenczi married Gizella in 1919, when he is 46 and Gizella 55 years old.

The importance of the analysis of the correspondence between the two men lies in the understanding of their emotional and historical contexts. It provides a new understanding of the concrete facts related to their life history during this turbulent historic period and, at the same time, contributes to the understanding of the theoretical developments of psychoanalysis as a fundamental basis of the further developments of the psychoanalytic theory. It is possible to glimpse the nature of their relationship, both academic and personal, and their conception on different topics, such as the political and social sphere of their time, the academic circles and academic publishing, the psychological impact that of the war on their psyche and of their families and friends, as well as their intellectual referents and theoretical productions.

The theoretical contributions of psychoanalysis, as well as the historical context and the transformation of classical theories to more contemporary theories, allows deepening in the extensive work and contributions of Sándor Ferenczi. These fundamental contributions have many times been left aside or have not been given the credit that they truly deserve. His *personae*, his friendship with Freud and the series of advances and theoretical contributions are the fundamental basis from which many future conceptualizations of psychoanalytic thought and technique emerge. The understandings of these issues are still fruitful for the current practice of contemporary psychoanalysts and clinicians.

Chapter 4

# Ferenczi as a translator and divulgater of Freud's work

The Budapest Psychoanalytic Society was officially created in May 19, 1913, having Sándor Ferenczi as its president until his death in 1933. István Hollós served as its vice president and Sándor Radó as secretary. Other important members were Anton von Freund, Lajos Levy (who was married to von Freund's sister (Weibel, 2005, p. 529)) and the renowned poet Hugo Ignotus. This shows the diverse disciplines that were represented in the members of the school and how it was not only a medical fief. Psychoanalysis was at the core of Hungary's intellectual crucible during the 20th century. As mentioned by Stanton (1997), "[s]een from the outside, the Society appears quite subversive, as it contains vociferous and renowned supporters of world communism, gay rights, antimilitarism and the impending collapse of the Habsburg empire" (p. 22). Meanwhile, Ignotus was an editor of the *Nyugat* (*"The West"*) journal, which had great influence in the Hungarian literature, to the point that writer Desző Kosztolányi (1855–1936) began his career as a poet in that journal.

The year 1918 was very important for the psychoanalytic movement in Hungary, for it was in that year that the V Psychoanalytic Congress in Budapest took place. Its main topic was the clinic of "war neuroses," which was especially relevant in the aftermath of the trench wars of WWI, which had ended a year before. The display of the congress and its reception by different sectors of society (politicians, doctors, intellectuals, artists, etc.) was of such magnitude, that Freud (2002/1918, p. 382) wrote to Karl Abraham (1877–1925)

DOI: 10.4324/9780367854355-4

that probably Budapest would be the world capital of psycho-analysis. In 1918, the Budapest Society had twenty members. Von Freund had a very key role in the organization and display of the Psychoanalytic Congress, for he financed most aspects of the organization. Von Freund was a rich entrepreneur, who had studied chemistry and was the owner of the important brewery Kőbányai. He not only financed most of the congress, but he also gave resources for the creation of a bookstore, an editorial and a psychoanalytic clinic (Danto, 2005, p. 21–24). Due to the political convulsions in the following years, both the library and the book-store were finally established in Vienna in 1920.

Nonetheless, the war did limit the amount of attendees to the Congress (forty-two people in total), but it was still thought of a great success for the psychoanalytic movement. Being mostly a marginal movement, it was received with great splendour, having authorities from Austria, Germany and Hungary present in the opening ceremony, being officially greeted by the Major of the city, and the involvement of local newspapers, medical journals and even the Academy of Sciences (Jiménez Avello, 1998, p. 139–40).

Ferenczi's important social and cultural influence continued growing.

> Ferenczi was strongly involved in the coffee-house culture of the Budapest intelligentsia, and, specifically, in the modernist avant-garde circles in Budapest [...] He maintained friendship with leading literary figures [...]. Under his influence several famous poets underwent therapeutic analysis (Moreau-Ricaud, 1996, 2012). Modernist literary forums disseminated psychoanalysis, which became popular in lay upper circles. Ferenczi rightly wrote to Freud in 1912 that 'analytic fever hit Budapest' (cited by Moreau-Ricaud, 1996, p. 50). Thus, Ferenczi became a catalyst not only for the international psychoanalytic movement, but also for the cross-fertilization of psychoanalysis and wider Hungarian culture (Mészáros, 2012). (Szokolszky, 2016, p. 24)

The Congress in Budapest concurred with a socialist and liberal revolution that took power in Hungary in October, 1918.

The government officials were curious in the new science of psychoanalysis and many of them attended the event. Many of them were interested in the possible treatments for war neuroses. Some Jewish intellectuals close to psychoanalysis were part of the government, such as psychoanalyst Jenő Varga, appointed commissar of finance, and philosopher György Lukács, elected as commissar of culture.

A few months later, a communist revolution will seize power for 133 days. This will also benefit the psychoanalytic movement in Hungary, for it led to Ferenczi's appointment as the first professor of psychoanalysis in a university.

> The liberal government was sympathetic to reforms in higher education, and when medical students demanded in a petition that Ferenczi get an academic position at the Pázmány University, a nomination procedure started. The university council was against it, but after the communist take-over the Bolshevist government granted Ferenczi a professorship and approved the establishment of a Department of Psychoanalysis against the will of the Council of the Medical Faculty (Erős, 2009, 2011, Mészáros, 1998, Moreau-Ricaud, 1996). At a time when psychoanalysis was at the periphery of international academic life and nowhere in the world was it present in universities, the short-lived Hungarian Soviet Republic presented an unprecedented opportunity for psychoanalysis to establish itself as an academic discipline. (Szokolszky, 2016, p. 26)

The "Galileo Group." conformed mostly by doctors and medical students, and who had attended to Ferenczi's lectures, led the initiative of gathering a large amount of signatures to request the creation of a course on psychoanalysis in the Medicine Faculty and a Psychoanalytic Department at Pázmány University directed by none other than Sándor Ferenczi. The first petition, presented in 1918, was rejected. However, the following year, when Béla Kun served as president of the Soviet Republic of Hungary, the petition was approved. The approval was also signed by Lukács, who was not especially fond of psychoanalysis. The approval of this request made of Ferenczi the first professor of psychoanalysis in a university and it is the first time in history that psychoanalysis had an official chair in the university. Students of the course were even allowed to have clinical practices at the Baticzfalvi Sanatorium in Budapest. In addition, at this time, Géza Róheim was named the first professor of anthropology and Révész the first professor of experimental psychology (Stanton, 1997, p. 29), all thanks to the revolutionary transformation of the university, which was being led by Lukács. However, the political outburst that would follow did not allow sustaining this ideal state of affairs. The rise to power of Miklós Horthy, the expedition of anti-Semitic measures and the extent of the "white terror," led Ferenczi, as well as Révész, to lose their positions in the university. What followed was the emigration of many Hungarian psycho-analyst to other countries, amongst them Sándor Radó, Jenő Hárnik, Jenő Varga, Sándor Lóránd and also Melanie Klein, who had become a member of the Budapest psychoanalytic society in 1919. Others, such as Róbert Bak, David Rapaport, Mihály and Alice Bálint, Franz Alexander and Teréz Benedek, would promptly follow.

In the following chapters, we will look deeper into some of Ferenczi's key concepts, as well as to the highlights of his relation to Freud and to the psychoanalytic movement, those which led to his exclusion from the history of psychoanalysis, as well as to his consecration as a fundamental hinge in the future of the science of the unconscious.

# Chapter 5

# The concept of "Introjection"

The first reference to Ferenczi's article "Transference and Introjection" (1909) can be found in 1908 in the Ferenczi–Freud correspondence. It is a time when both analysts have an interest in the relationship between paranoia and projection. However, there are certain doubts on the part of Freud as to whether or not "introjection" would be a valid concept for psychoanalysis.

In 1909, there are still no technical works on the topic of transference. There are some comments in "Study on hysteria" (1895) and in "Fragment of analysis of a case of hysteria" (1905). Furthermore, the concept of "transference" has been used in the *Interpretation of dreams* (1900) and, until that moment, it has to do with repressed tendencies that were revived in the relationship with the analyst; people significantly important to the analysand were transferred on to the person of the doctor. It was understood as a resistance insofar as it functioned in opposition to remembrance. It meant a shift of the affects onto the person of the doctor. The willingness to transfer was already there and the psychoanalytic framework gave it the opportunity to unfold. The concept of "transference neuroses" had not yet made its appearance.

Agustín Genovés (1998) highlights the difficulty in reading this article given Ferenczi's internal debate in elaborating and sustaining Freudian ideas and, at the same time, his own. It allows us to think about Ferenczi's own transference with his mentor. Freud seems to be clear about what is happening to his disciple and tells

DOI: 10.4324/9780367854355-5

him in a letter in October 21, 1908: "You are anxiously trying to confirm me. If you abandon this intention, you will find a rich material from which the confirmations will emerge in the end" (quoted by Genovés, p. 63).

Ferenczi (1909) proposes a broader definition of transference: "transference is a psychical mechanism that is characteristic of the neurosis altogether, one that is evidenced in all situations of life, and which underlies most of the pathological manifestations" (p. 36). It can therefore be seen that it ranges from the psycho-pathological manifestations of hysteria (hysterical identification, hysterical disturbances of physiological functions and conversion symptoms), to those of obsessive neuroses (excessive behaviours of neurotics, "altruistic" social manifestations that are product of displacements of repressed selfish tendencies). In this way, the article blurs the boundaries between displacement and transference. Ferenczi clarifies that he is aware of having used both terms synonymously and says that transference is only a particular case of the general tendency of neurotics towards transference; that is to say, the displacement would be the general mechanism and transference a particular aspect of it. However, as the article continues, the concepts seem to be confused once again. He says

> When we bear in mind these different varieties of the transference to the physician, we become decidedly strengthened in our assumption that this is only one manifestation, although in a practical way the most important one, of the general neurotic *passion for transference*. This passion, or mania, we may regard as the most fundamental peculiarity of the neuroses, and also that which goes most to explain their conversion and substitution symptoms." (p. 45)

Genovés indicates that this confusion seems to be the product of the fact that at that time there is no clarity in the theory of the distinction between the Freudian idea of intrapsychic transference and clinical transference. In "Study on hysteria" (1895) and *The Interpretation of Dreams* (1900), Freud describes the transference of unconscious desires to the remains of the day and the transference of intensities from one representation to another and it seems to be the sense in which the term is used by Ferenczi. The author goes on to explain, relying on the economic point of view, how (primary) repression leads to the splitting of the representations from the affects and this "freely floating affect" would be the origin of the anxiety and the production of symptoms. This produces certain discussions with Freud as reflected in the letters of February 13 and 16, 1910. What can be read, however, in what Ferenczi exposes, is that repression liberates a *quantum* of libido from its corresponding representations and that, since this situation becomes intolerable (given a psyche that works by the pleasure principle), it will tend to neutralize it by linking it to other representations, be them somatic, as in the conversion syndromes, or mental, as in obsessive neuroses. However, there will always be a residue that is what generates the transference: "The idea of this excitation could be used to explain the neurotic passion for transference, and be made responsible for the "manias" of the neurotic. (In the *petite hystérie* these manias seem to constitute the essence of the disease)" (p. 46). Genovés points out that this particularity dissolves the ambiguity of the term according to which it would explain most of the conversion and substitution symptoms, presenting instead the transference as that portion of libido that turns to the outside world in search of objects to neutralize the excitement. Ferenczi finds this residual libido as the basis for the concepts of transference and introjection, which give his article its title. The transference is directed towards an object and introjection towards the inclusion in the self: "Whereas the paranoiac expels from his ego the impulses that have become unpleasant, the neurotic helps himself by taking into the ego as large as possible a part of the outer world, making it the object of unconscious phantasies. This is a kind of diluting process, by means of which he tries to mitigate the poignancy of free-floating, unsatisfied, and unsatisfiable, unconscious wish-impulses. One might give to this process, in contrast to projection, the name of *Introjection*" (p. 48).

Genovés (1998) affirms that introjection (*intro* – in, *yectare* – throw) is an "amoeboid movement that encompasses something from the outside world within the self. Introjection seeks to re-establish with objects from the outside world an economic equilibrium that has been disturbed by repression" (p. 68). This double movement suggests that not only a defence mechanism is at stake, but also a certain need to inscribe something from the outside world into the psyche. Genovés thinks of it as a kind of "representational void," pure "floating libido" that goes out to meet external objects to introject them.

In some moments, Ferenczi seems to corroborate Freud's assertion that the analyst acts by mere presence, unleashing something that was already preformed, but in others he goes on to describe what he calls the "real" aspects of the analyst. This will be a topic of great importance in the later developments of his theory, when he highlights more these "real" traits of the analyst and the technical modifications regarding the effects of the psychoanalytic setting.

In a later article entitled "The concept of introjection" (1912), Ferenczi affirms that paranoid patients who can retain some interest in the outside world are of better prognosis, for they can introject and retain a certain relationship with the outside world. This would place them closer to neurotics and give them a better clinical prognosis. With this, he explains more clearly that the potentiality of transference in the analysis is played on having or not the capacity to introject.

Another very important point to highlight of "Transference and introjection" is the explanation given to the origin of the differentiation of the subject from the external world (object). Ferenczi starts from the idea of an original monism to explain a primitive introjection and projection. Initially, the child does not distinguish between an internal and an external stimulus, but this will be a later process of the experience. This primitive introjection and projection suggest a reflection on how the psyche accesses reality. It is interesting to see in his approach something of what Freud later called "initial ego/reality" and "purified-pleasure-ego" in "Instincts and their vicissitudes" (1915) and "definitive real self" in "Denial" (1925). Ferenczi (1909) says

> We may suppose that to the new-born child everything perceived by the senses appears unitary, so to speak monistic. Only later does he learn to distinguish from his ego the

malicious things, forming an outer world that does not obey his will. That would be the first projection process, the primordial projection, and the later paranoiac probably makes use of the path thus traced out, in order to expel still more of his ego into the outer world. A part of the outer world, however, greater or less, is not so easily cast off from the ego, but continually obtrudes itself again on the latter, challenging it, so to speak; "Fight with me or be my friend" (Wagner, Gotterdammerung, Act I). If the individual has unsettled affects at his disposal, and these he soon has, he accepts this challenge by extending his "interest" from the ego on to the part of the outer world. The first loving and hating is a transference of auto-erotic pleasant and unpleasant feelings on to the objects that evoke those feelings. The first "object-love" and the first "object-hate" are, so to speak, the primordial transferences, the roots of every future introjection (p. 49).

It is clear to see that here there is an extension of Freud's ideas on transference. For Freud, transference implies both a constituted psychic apparatus, as a primary repression, a content that refers to the oedipal situation and the expression of a forgotten past. For Ferenczi, transference is the cause and is contemporary to the constitution of the psychic apparatus; therefore, it would not be just a phenomenon of repetition. Genovés highlights at this point the discussion regarding child analysis (which will become visceral in the future of psychoanalysis between Anna Freud and Melanie Klein). If transference is the repetition of a forgotten past and its content is oedipal, then it would not be possible to analyse a child until he had passed through Oedipus and primary repression. Ferenczi, on the contrary, conceptualizes a transference that displays from the origin of psychic life. There is a clear influence of Ferenczi's ideas on introjection on the later work of his former analysand, Melanie Klein. In Kleinian theory, in the origins of psychic activity, a pure death drive prevails. Before the first expulsion there is an increase in tension in the psychic apparatus, followed by an expulsion of that excess into the world. A first introjection occurs (which constitutes the first introjected object) that will be the starting point for the function of the superego. This first expulsion of the death drive links with an object. The object, which is damaged, is thus introjected by the apparatus. The persecutory anxiety leads to an increase in tension in the apparatus and leads to a second moment of projection (which does not constitute, in itself, an expulsion). Thus, the outside world is cathected and a psychic reality is built. Klein refers to imagos, phantasmatic nuclei that are covered by introjections. The first imagos correspond to Freud's proto-phantasies: seduction, castration and sadistic sexual intercourse. That which is persecutory of these imagos is expelled and stains the outside world. These imagos are full of anxiety, but there is a representation for that anxiety. On the contrary, the anni-hilation anxiety lacks representation; it is anxiety without an object. The representative of the death drive in Klein's theory is sadism. The imagos, together with a remnant of the death drive that remained unexpelled, constitute the core of the superego. Both the internal and external world are invested with fantasies and as long as these exist, the psychic apparatus can function. In her clinical work with children, Klein observed the conflict that arises when playing stops and cannot continue (putting an end to the use of play in its analogous function to adult's free associa-tion). If the process of introjection and projection continue ap-propriately, the anxiety may lead towards a depressive anxiety. Finally, Klein also refers to a breast that is undamaged by the suction orality, which implies an identification free of sadism, which would be the one against which primary envy would be directed. This Kleinian conceptualization clearly echoes these aspects of Ferenczian theory.

The second part of "Transference and introjection" is entitled "Role of transference in hypnosis and suggestion." Ferenczi is interested in exploring the relationships between hypnosis and suggestion in transference (transference links these two con-cepts). Transference does not belong only to the psychoanalytic field, but has an application to a broader field. Suggestibility, present both in hypnosis and in suggestion, is an expression of the disposition to transference, which displays the repressed infantile representations through the figure of the analyst or the hypnotist. Ferenczi differentiates psychoanalysis from other techniques by saying that while the latter seek to reinforce and cultivate the transference, the former is dedicated to unmasking what it hides, dissolving it. His formulations, moreover, deprive the hypnotist of the powers that are commonly attributed to him, such as exercising his will over that of the patient. Instead, he states that it is the patient who is active

> If we now imagine from this aspect the psychical state of a person to whom something is to be suggested, we note a displacement of the earlier point of view, a displacement that is of cardinal importance. The unconscious mental forces of the 'medium' appear as the real active agent, whereas the hypnotist, previously pictured as all-powerful, has to content himself with the part of an object used by the unconscious of the apparently unresisting 'medium' according to the latter's individual and temporary disposition. (p. 60)

Later, Ferenczi affirms that, like Freud, he considers that credulity and docility in the hypnotic state have their origin in the masochistic tendencies of the sexual drive and affirms that "hypnosis is nothing other than the transitory regression to the phase of submission, credulity and childish abandonment." He suggests two methods to hypnotize: one would be the paternal or intimidating and, the other, maternal or tender. Here we find the germ of what will be his theory about trauma, for example in what is exposed in "Confusion of tongues between the adult and the child" (1933), where the idea of passionate punishments or excessive tenderness appears as a pathological expression of the repressed sexuality of the adult.

In 1913, Ferenczi presented at the APA Congress in Munich an article entitled "Faith, credulity and conviction from the point of view of Medical Psychology." In it, he argues that he observes a resistance in patients who show excessive enthusiasm and faith in the treatment that leads them to blindly accept all the analyst's interpretations in order to ensure lost parental affection. Thus, in the manner of a positive transference, a deeper desire is hidden that aspires to be fulfilled. The origin of this is in childhood. Once the child has lost his original omnipotence, and afflicted by an external world that does not work according to his wishes, he begins to transfer his omnipotence fantasies to the adult. This aspect of his theory of transference will be of great interest to French psychoanalyst Jacques Lacan in his conceptualization of the "Subject Supposed to Know", which refers to the effect of transference through which the analysand attributes a knowledge about himself to the analyst, being the analyst the bearer of what the analysand ignores about himself (the analyst endures this position, though he knows it is not he who knows, but the analysand, yet the analysand does not know that he knows, that is, that the knowledge he seeks about himself lies within him, in his unconscious, and not in the analyst).

Ferenczi affirms that education plays an important role and can lead to confuse the child by imposing certain guidelines and beliefs that, many times, contradict what the child perceives and interprets. Despite what his own judgment dictates, the child renounces to it in order to satisfy his dependency needs and to be able to continue keeping the adult in a place of omnipotence. This is an important antecedent of what will be his trauma theory and what he will later conceptualize in "The adaptation of the family to the child" (1928).

In this way, hypnosis would be nothing more than that regression to "the phase of submission, credulity and childhood abandonment" (Ferenczi, 1909). In transference, the infantile need to illusively revive that lost infantile omnipotence is recreated. "It would then be the loss of the feeling of one's own omnipotence without renouncing to the belief in its existence that determines the transfer of these fantasies on the significant adult in the hope of recovering it through him" (Genovés. 1998, p. 78). With this, Ferenczi contributes to the nascent theory of transference and to the concept of introjection.

To conclude, it is possible to affirm that the idea of transference as the need to satisfy infantile sexual desires is taken further by articulating the idea of freely floating affects that have been stripped of their representation (as a result of repression) in search of new ties, being the person of the analyst a privileged one for these purposes. In addition to infantile sexual desires, Ferenczi introduces the desires to regain omnipotence, which is something that would be inscribed in the narcissistic needs of the subject. The concept of introjection, apart from accounting for the operation of the transference, accounts for a fundamental mechanism for the construction of the psyche.

# Chapter 6

# Ferenczi's introduction of technical innovations

From the earliest moments in his relation with psychoanalysis, Ferenczi was fascinated and intrigued by technique. He had studied Breuer's cathartic method and witnessed its effects in his consultation room, as well as Jung's "Word Association Test." He then became a rigorous apprentice of Freudian technique and evidenced its therapeutic effects. But he was also questioned by the results of those treatments that did not have the effects he expected through the use of standard techniques. As many of Freud's pupils, he looked for possible changes in the technique in order to reduce the duration of analysis. On occasions, as Rank and Freud did in certain moments (as in the case of the "Wolf Man," 1918), he set a term for the termination of the analysis, but later he took distance from this as a viable tool for intervention.

Since 1919, Ferenczi produced a series of articles and lectures regarding the matter of technique, which would continue to be a persistent subject of thought and research for him. The titles of these articles speak for themselves: "On the Technique of Psycho-Analysis" (1919), "Technical Difficulties in the Analysis of a Case of Hysteria" (1919), "The Further Development of an Active Therapy in Psycho-Analysis" (1920) and "Contra-indications to the 'Active' Psycho-Analytical Technique" (1925) are some of the most suggestive ones.

His first most explicit and documented technical innovation was that which he termed the "active technique." Through it, he intended to produce an increase in tension in the analytic treatment,

DOI: 10.4324/9780367854355-6

triggering emotional and cognitive effects in the patient that put the analysis in course there were there seemed to be a stagnation of its course.

Ferenczi was open to the unleashing of negative transference in the patient towards the analyst and believed it was important for the patient to be able to express it and make it explicit during the analytic treatment. He saw that many times the patients did not dare to speak about it, even though they felt profoundly dissatisfied with the treatment and the analyst. He even encouraged his colleagues to recognize their mistakes, if there were, to the patient, giving primacy to honesty and authenticity over authority and medical hypocrisy.

Ferenczi, as the great clinician he was, learned from his own keen clinical practice that technique is not a box into which you have to force every patient, and that if it does not work for them it is because of the patient's fault, but instead he found out that many times it was necessary to introduce modifications on the classic techniques and, we could think even more extremely, that each patient could require certain unique technical specifications. "In the course of my practical analytical work, which extended over many years, I constantly found myself infringing one or another of Freud's injunctions in his 'Recommendations on Technique'. For instance, my attempt to adhere to the principle that patients must be in a lying position during analysis would at times be thwarted by their uncontrollable impulse to get up and walk about the room or speak to me face to face. Or again, difficulties in the real situation, and often the unconscious machinations of the patient, would leave me with no alternative but either to break off the analysis or to depart from the general rule and carry it on without remuneration. I did not hesitate to adopt the latter alternative—not without success. The principle that the patient should be analysed in his ordinary environment and should carry on his usual occupation, was very often impossible to enforce. In some severe cases I was even obliged to let patients stay in bed for days and weeks and to relieve them of the effort of coming to my house. The sudden breaking-off of the analysis at the end of the hour very often had the effect of a shock, and I would be forced to prolong the treatment until the reaction had spent itself; sometimes I had to devote two or more hours a day to a single patient" (Ferenczi, 1931b, p. 114). So, in recumbence or face to face, sessions of one hour or more, treatments in the analyst's office or in the patient's house, with or without payment, etc., are all relative to the logic and specific aspects of the treatment and not something that can be prescribed as a generality to which all patients (and analysts!) have to adhere to. As we know from different sources (Lohser & Newton, 1996), and as Ferenczi made explicit, Freud was not himself an orthodox and what he stated in "Recommendations on technique" "were really intended only as warnings for beginners and [a] considerable scope was left for the exercise of the analyst's own judgement" (Ferenczi, 1931b, p. 115). Ferenczi encourages the analyst to intervene not only guided by the "principle of frustration," that is, frustrating the patient in his wishes and infantile desires, but also by the "principle of indulgence." This is what makes each time more crucial the analysis of the analyst: the analyst must have clear if when he intervenes he is acting in the benefit of the analysand's analysis and not in the unconscious satisfaction of his sadistic or masochistic impulses.

In the case of the active technique, Ferenczi discovers that one of his patients crosses her legs in the couch, incurring in a masturbatory stimulation, and through it reducing the tension in the analytic session. To mobilize that tension, Ferenczi actively instructs her to not cross her legs. "When I told a patient, whose habit it was to cross her legs, that she must not do so, I was actually creating a situation of libidinal frustration, which induced a heightening of tension and the mobilization of psychic material hitherto repressed" (Ferenczi, 1929, p. 115). But later he makes use of a different technique, inviting the patient to relax her extremities and abandon her physical stiffness and the rigidity of her extremities. He believes these to be the two main techniques of psycho-analysis, the active technique and the relaxation and neocatharsis technique: "psycho-analysis employs two opposite methods: it produces heightening of tension by the frustration it imposes and relaxation by the freedom it allows" (Ferenczi, 1929, p. 115). By neocatharsis, Ferenczi meant that he was not merely returning to Breuer's cathartic method, but allowing to produce for the first time, in analysis, that which the patient was deprived from in his earliest infancy. Certain very early experiences occurred when the child's cognitive and memory functions were not fully developed, leaving impressions in the body, but not being evoked through thought. The technical innovations proposed by Ferenczi would allow the patient to have an Ego experience of that which happened in his life before a fully constituted Ego and, sometimes due to severe trauma, existed in a split off part of the personality, but was not incorporated in the subject's experience as a whole. It will be later that he will introduce a third psychoanalytic techniquthe Catholic Church. Relations betweene, named in his *Clinical Diary* as "mutual analysis." We will disclose it thoroughly in Chapter 11, "Splitting as a psychic defence."

Ferenczi pioneered the introduction of modifications in analytic technique. He observed that not all patients accommodated the analytical device in the same way. As an "expert in difficult cases," as he made himself known (Ferenczi, 1984/1931), he knew about psychosis and the need to approach it differently from traditional cases. It is his own passion for the unconscious, its possibilities of deciphering and its limits, which led him to introduce modifications in the technique as attempts to get hold of what was presented to him in the clinical experience, which insisted in it and which, at the same time, eluded him.

As mentioned before, in the chapter regarding "The end of analysis," French Psychoanalyst Jacques Lacan found in Ferenczi "the most pertinent of the first-generation authors to question what was required of an analyst, especially in regard to the end of treatment" (Lacan, 1955, cited by Lugrin, 2017). After the IPA prohibited Lacan to continue his training of analysts, and his forthcoming demission from the IPA (which led to one of the most dramatic divisions within the psychoanalytic movement of all times), he referred to this experience as his "excomulgation" (Lacan, 1964/1998) and identified in this condition of being banned from the official institution with Baruch Spinoza's experience with the Catholic Church. Relations between the two analysts can also be traced to the IPA's silent veto on Ferenczi's writings. In his 1953 seminar, Lacan said that: "Ferenczi was to some extent considered, up to 1930, to be the *enfant terrible* of psychoanalysis. In relation to the analytic group in general, he remained a freewheeler. His way of raising questions showed no concern for couching itself in a manner which was, at that time, already *orthodox*" (Lacan, 1975, p. 208). In an important article entitled "The function of the field of speech and language in Psychoanalysis" (which is commonly referred to as the "Rome Discourse") he said that "psychoanalysts who are also mothers, even those who give our loftiest deliberations a ma-triarchal air, are not exempt from that confusion of tongues by which Ferenczi designated the law of the relationship between the child and the adult" (Lacan, 1953, p. 36, cited by Barzilai, 1997, p. 568). Barzilai also cites Lacan's "further praises [for] Ferenczi for posing 'the question of the analyst's being… very early in the history of analysis,' and thereby introducing 'the problem of analytic action' almost 50 years before in an essay entitled 'Introjection and Transference'" (1909) and that "anticipated by a long way all the themes later developed about this topic" (Lacan, 1958, p. 250, cited by Barzilai, 1997, p. 568). Nonetheless, in other parts of his seminars he criticizes Ferenczi's excessive emphasis on developmental stages, which even though is present in his early psychoanalytic writings, does not constitute the core or main contributions (definitely not the most original) of his work.

A key anticipation which may be found in his *Clinical Diary* and in "Notes and Fragments" is an early conceptualization of the traumatic core in language itself, which will later be displayed in depth in Lacan and in post-Lacanian analysts through the concepts of the "Real," "*troumatisme*" and "*lalange.*" While describing the psychic functioning of his patients in analysis, Ferenczi mentions that "If the intellectual *cs* [conscious] urge to communicate is completely eliminated and the speech organs are given free reign… there comes—after senseless vowels and consonants (as in the play of infants with lips and tongue) imitations of things, animals, and people" (p. 265). Etymologically, *infans* refers to he who does not speak. That primordial aspect of the subject before being captured by the language apparatus is of great interest for Ferenczi and Lacan. For Lacan, there is no subject outside of language: at the same time, humans exist in language and are pre-existed by language. Nonetheless, for Lacan, the function of language is not only for communication, for there is enjoyment (*jouissance*) in the experience of language and this is evidenced in Lacan's thoughts on the child's babbling, not as a prelanguage (as suggested by evolutionary psychologists, such as Jean Piaget), but as a form of enjoyment in language itself before it is completely taken by the symbolic functions of speech. But the non-symbolic (or non-symbolized) aspects of language continue existing throughout a mature language and coexist with the other functions of language.

For Ferenczi, on the other hand, the transformation produced by language is severe but not absolute and the aspects of the psyche not captured by language seem to continue having an influence and function in the mental lives of adults: "By carrying over into biology this piece of insight gained in the psychic sphere, it is possible for us to think of coitus and sleep as the conducting off of current traumatic stimuli and, at the same time, the expression of the striving to reproduce the intrauterine and thalassal situation seemingly long since transcended—nay, we could even perceive in them a return to still more archaic and primitive strivings towards repose (impulse towards the inorganic state, death impulse)" (Ferenczi, 1924/1968, p. 85).

Regressive states, such as sleep or madness, can lead the psyche to those primordial states: "Sleep is regression to a primordial unity, as yet unsplit. (Without consciousness and, when completely without objects, dreamless). Regression to the pretraumatic" (Ferenczi, 1932, p. 113). As stated by Gutiérrez-Peláez (2015), in Ferenczi's final writings, psychoanalysis has to do with the healing of a primordial trauma, an *Urtrauma*: "Through analysis of his patients, Ferenczi intended to reach the human order before language itself, an order linked with the universe, the inorganic, with an absence of splitting and an access to the 'language of the organs' (Ferenczi, 1933/1955d, pp. 6–7), or the 'anarchy of the organs' (pp. 69–70)" (Gutiérrez-Peláez, 2015, p. 150). Despite this diverging roads, they nonetheless lead to a common ground, which is the need to introduce technical innovations in psychoanalysis. The work with very disturbed patients (with "cleavage pathologies" according to Jimenez-Avello's (2018) terminology), makes it necessary to face the limits of the classic settings in order to overcome the obstacles during the analysis. It also requires a well-analysed analyst who is aware of his limits and has delved deeply into his own unconscious, so he can be sufficiently alert when these technical innovations are resistential (introduced to avoid leading to unknown and anxiety-producing parts of his psyche) and when there are truly for the benefit of the patient and within the ethics of psychoanalysis.

We have described Ferenczi's technical innovations in former chapters. Lacan's innovations had to do with introducing a punctuation (*ponctuation*) through the abrupt finishing of the psychoanalytic session, which aimed to avoid that the patient intellectualized an unconscious formation (such as a *lapsus linguae*), filling it with sense during the rest of the session. The abrupt termination of the session (which is not arbitrary, but calculated within the logic of the session and of the treatment) allowed leaving the unconscious "open" and intensifying the patient's own experience of his or her unconscious. As stated by Evans (2006), these technique "has been a source of controversy throughout the history of Lacanian psychoanalysis, since it contravenes the traditional IPA practice of sessions of fixed duration. Lacan's practice of sessions of variable duration (Fr. *Séances scandées*—wrongly dubbed 'short sessions' by his critics) came to be one of the main reasons that the IPA gave for excluding him when the SFP was negotiating for IPA recognition in the early 1960s. Today, the technique of punctuation, especially as expressed in the practice of sessions of variable duration, continues to be a distinctive feature of Lacanian psychoanalysis" and which led eventually to the creation of his dissident school of psychoanalysis, today most clearly embraced by the *World Association of Psychoanalysis*[1]. It was this technical innovation that eventually lead to Lacan's "excomulgation," as were Ferenczi's technical innovations which probably weighted most heavily in his banning from the history of the psychoanalytic movement. Nonetheless, it was probably Lacan's determination and strong spirit that did not allow his ideas to be buried alive or forcefully disappeared.

## Ferenczi's ideas on psychoanalytic innovations and technique in his correspondence with Freud

While Ferenczi is working on his own original ideas on theory and technique, he continues to be an active member of the psychoanalytic movement and endures sustaining an active correspondence with Freud. In his letters, Ferenczi speaks enthusiastically of Anna Freud's (Sigmund Freud's daughter) entry into the psychoanalytic society. He also makes explicit to Freud his work on the technique of psychoanalysis: "The hours are still fun for me, in part; to be sure, I now seem to be less focused on finding new things than I am on achieving better results with improvement in technique" (p. XIX). This is a clear indication that he would dedicate himself to improving his technique for the rest of his life. This technique was also the basis for undertaking experiments that would precipitate disagreements between him and Freud, as well as with other members of the psychoanalytic community.

Many times in their letters Freud and Ferenczi talk about Ferenczi's developments in the "active therapy" or "technique" with which Freud disagrees. Ferenczi tells his colleague that he feels more and more sure of his technique and satisfied with its therapeutic results. In other moments, as in his article "Child-Analysis in the Analysis of Adults" (1931), Ferenczi describes his unorthodox way of working: "Not infrequently patients, often in the middle of their free associations, produce little stories which they have made up, or even poems and rhymes, and sometimes they ask for a pencil so as to make us a present of a drawing, generally of a very naïve sort. Naturally I let them indulge in this and make the little gifts a starting-point for further fantasy-formations, which I afterwards analyse. Does not this by itself sound as if it came from the analysis of children?" (p. 133). Regarding the duration of the sessions, Ferenczi mentions that "[t]he analytic session is prolonged till the emotions roused by the material are composed" (Ferenczi, 1931, p. 137). Regarding touching patients, he mentions: "Tactful and calming words, reinforced perhaps by an encouraging pressure of the hand, or, if that is not enough, a friendly stroking of the patient's head [...]" (Ferenczi, 1931, p. 138). In the same article, a few lines after, he mentions: "My excuse is that I did not bring about this process intentionally: it developed as the result of what I considered a legitimate attempt to enhance the freedom of association. I have a certain respect for such spontaneous reactions; I therefore let them appear without hindrance, and I surmise that they manifest tendencies to reproduction which should not, in my opinion, be inhibited, but should be brought to full development before we try to master them" (Ferenczi, 1931, p. 139).

Initially, Ferenczi expected to shorten the analysis through his technical innovations of relaxation and neocatharsis. Nonetheless, with time he becomes more sceptical about this, but did not disregard them as useless. Even though they probably do not make analysis shorter, they do lead us to a deeper understanding of the human mind and the effects they produce can have a more consistent permanence: "I must confess two things; that my hope of considerably *shortening* the analysis by the help of relaxation and catharsis has, so far, not been fulfilled, and that this method has made the analyst's work considerably more laborious. But what it has done—and I trust will do still more—is to deepen our insight into the workings of the human mind in health and in disease and to entitle us to hope that any therapeutic success achieved, being based on these deeper foundations, will have a better prospect of permanence" (Ferenczi, 1931, p. 141).

## Growing disagreements in the Freud-Ferenczi correspondence

The third volume of the Freud-Ferenczi correspondence begins in the aftermath of World War I. In these letters, the following main topics can be highlighted: Groddeck's appearance and his meeting with Ferenczi; Freud's disease; the disagreements between Freud, Ferenczi and Rank; Ferenczi's trip to the USA; and the emotional crisis between Freud and Ferenczi.

Freud and Ferenczi discuss frequently the economic difficulties of the psychoanalytic movement. After the death of Anton von Freund ("Toni") on January 20, 1920, the psychoanalytic movement had to look carefully into its economical aspects, for von Freund was an important source of income for the movement. The event left them deeply saddened and the letters of this moment revolve around the friendship they had with their colleague and what his departure left behind. Freud wrote an obituary for von Freund a few days after (Freud, 1920). Freud and Ferenczi spoke about the use of "11,000 crowns" (Falzelder & Barant, p. 4) to support a psychoanalytic society and the "St. Stephen's Corp" which was intended to be sold and the intervention of both analusts was needed for this. Ferenczi told Freud about his busy situation regarding the economy in Budapest and his long working hours that did not allow him to do any other intellectual work. At moments Ferenczi talks about the troubles in Budapest arguing that the bad weather (floods and crops) has caused a bad financial situation at a global level which has led to several suicides in the population. They also speak about the financial situation of the psychoanalytic journals *Verlag* and *Imago*. In certain moments, their economic situation is difficult, but in others, their commercial success is highlighted. It is clear that, for both, these journals are key to the life and success of the psychoanalytic movement. Sometimes, more that the financial aspects, what puts them in danger are the political relations around the editorial committee and the rivalry and personal difficulties between the members of the societies.

Just a few days after the death of von Freund, Freud finds out about the death of his daughter Sophie because of the "Spanish influenza." She was expecting her third son at the moment of her death. Freud wrote to Ferenczi about his emotional situation related to the death of his daughter and how it has affected the family and, also, about his health which had declined and prevented him from working on the new editions of the "Theory of Sexuality" and "Jokes" (Falzelder & Barant, p. 13). From the 1920 on, the internal disputes of the psychoanalytic movement become each time more evident. Otto Rank, Ernest Jones, Eissler, Brill, among others, will be protagonists in the disputes to follow.

Ferenczi talked to Freud about a possible trip in Easter of 1920 to visit him. Within this process there is also Rank who was in charge of Ferenczi´s accommodation. Ferenczi sends Freud his text of *Elements of Psychoanalysis* and they talk in their correspondence of his mentors corrections to it. Freud mentions he believes the paper is suitable for the publication.

In May 30, 1920, Ferenczi wrote to Freud telling him about his "unpleasant depression" (Falzelder & Barant, p. 22) after being expelled of the "Physicians' Society of the Interior Ministry."

The Ministry expelled twenty-two people who had "compromised" themselves during the Council Republic. Ferenczi was upset with this and mentioned to Freud that "animosity toward psychoanalysis was certainly the reason why this treatment was accorded only to me" (p. 22), which makes evident how psychoanalysis, form its origins, has always been uncomfortable for the solidified institutions, as will be wonderfully expounded in Sándor Márai's obituary of Ferenczi. Many psychoanalyst left the country (among them Michael and Alice Bálint, and Franz Alexander), but Ferenczi decided to stay, encouraged by Freud, to prevent the downfall of psychoanalysis in Hungary.

In many moments in their correspondence, Freud and Ferenczi talk about their concerns regarding the health of their friend and their own. Ferenczi frequently asked Freud about his health, his discomfort and pain with the use of his prosthesis, and Freud as well was concerned with the health of his friend. Freud's concern for his old age is also evident. Ferenczi, on his behalf, had reported that his heart, aorta, kidneys and lungs were not healthy.

In 1920, it was first suggested that Ferenczi's ailment was a case of hypochondria, but eventually it seemed to progress into a more serious illness, until the final diagnosis of pernicious anaemia, which will be the determined cause of his death. Ferenczi talked about his intestinal disorders which he interprets as autoerotic compensation and highlights an introversion of libido, a characteristic that coined the term "pathoneuroses."

In February 10, 1920, Ferenczi wrote to Freud about the case of Eugénie Sokolnicka, a patient he began treating in Budapest in 1913. Sokolnicka had a very active paper in the expansion of psychoanalysis in France. In the letters, her analysis is bought up, and aspects of her case are discussed. They mention the monetary aspects about which the patient complained, since according to what was said, she interrupted the analysis when it was about to conclude. Sokolnicka brings together psychologists such as Adler, Jung, Freud and Ferenczi, since they all analysed this patient with negative results, and had reported that she was a very difficult patient. It was Ferenczi with whom the patient ended up feeling more comfortable and achieving more progress. Sokolnicka intended to travel to Paris and Freud and Ferenczi discuss the possibility of recommending her for the translation of the book *Interpretation of Dreams* to French (Falzelder & Barant, p. 44). Nonetheless her progress, Ferenczi was still concerned about her suicidal tendencies (she eventually killed herself in 1934). In the letters 863, 864 and 865 of their correspondence, Sokolnicka and Ferenczi's main clinical findings of her case continue to be discussed. The analysis of Sokolnicka is a very important issue at this time and Ferenczi and Freud talk about it in various letters. It is also evident how Ferenczi had a certain kind of "appreciation" for her for what she contributed to her self-discovery. It is until letter 866 when Freud tells Ferenczi that he has decided that he is not going to talk about the case anymore.

Another important female figure present in their correspondence is Princess Marie Bonaparte, who was analysed by Freud because of a case of frigidity. She eventually became his colleague, friend and pupil. She dedicated her life to psychoanalysis, translating some of Freud's works to French and being one of the most influential promoters of French psychoanalysis. It is also attributed to her the payment to the Nazi party to allow Freud's emigration to London.

An aspect of great importance revealed by their correspondence is the nature and direction of their relationship, as well as the function that each plays in the emotional and intellectual life of the other. Their letters become each time more personal. They talk about family matters, such as the eightieth birthday of Ferenczi's mother and the desire to spend Christmas with him. Ferenczi mentions: "You see: I don't want to give up the illusion that, despite the many changes –war- impoverishment- marital duties- it will still be possible to maintain our old summer meetings or trips" (Falzelder & Barant, p. 44). In *Letter 877*, Ferenczi reports on his mother's decline in health and her possible early death. In the next letter, her death is confirmed, leaving Ferenczi in a very difficult emotional position where he reports "hypnagogic hallucinations" (p. 61) that were characterized by the perception that the coffin was falling from the hearse, which he interprets psychoanalytically as an ambivalent fantasy where, on the one hand, there is the desire for revenge and, on the other, the desire for resurrection.

Many times the topics in their correspondence are not clinical or intellectual, but more personal. For example, the topic of Freud's birthdays appears year after year. In *Letter 853*, for example, Freud writes to Ferenczi about a coffee machine that Ferenczi gave him and about a surprise that someone revealed to Freud about a ring, which he asks to keep for his eightieth birthday. Ferenczi is planning Freud's birthday seven months in advance. Usually Ferenczi expresses his intent to surprise him and Freud expresses his antipathy towards birthday celebrations and the evidence of his old age, which brings the closeness of death.

Ferenczi writes to Freud about his interest in studying the psychoanalytical correlates of tics. He believes that it has a possible sensory-narcissistic origin and asks Freud's opinion on this idea. With this work, Ferenczi intends to identify the motor expressions in tics and catatonia, but he needs the aid of his colleague to help him land his ideas in a more solid clinical and theoretical ground. However, as he does in other moments, Freud decides not to give much opinion so as to favour the intellectual liberation of his colleague: "I am striving not to put anything in the way of your independence" (p. 38). Freud attempts to detach Ferenczi from his own ideas and opinions for what he himself calls the development of his independence. We will see that this is not always the case, and with respect to the lecture "Confusion of tongues between the adult and the child" (1932), Freud actively tries to discourage Ferenczi from presenting or publishing it.

## Ferenczi's relationship with Groddeck

Freud first met with George Groddeck in 1917 and later Ferenczi will also in 1921. Groddeck (1866–1934) was a German physician who was influenced by psychoanalysis for his developments in the field of psychosomatics and his work was credited by Freud for influencing his concept of the "Id" (Groddeck wrote a book entitled *The Book of the It* (1923); nonetheless, he was not what you would call an orthodox disciple of Freud). Groddeck had a significant influence in Ferenczi's life, who visited his sanatorium in Baden-Baden frequently. In addition to resting, Ferenczi visited the sanatorium with the purpose of studying the ideas and methods of his colleague and searching for his aid regarding personal matters. Their friend-ship lasted until the end of their lives. In their correspondence it is seen how Ferenczi narrates to Groddeck intimate matters. It is especially iconic his letter in Christmas 1921 where Ferenczi de-scribes personal aspects of his childhood and of his relationship with his parents.

After the Eleventh International Psychoanalytic Congress, Ferenczi felt affected by the high altitude in St. Moritz, for which he decided to spend some time in Groddeck's Sanatorium. It this con-gress Ferenczi presented key papers on his latest work, one regarding the "Advances in Analytic Technique" (later published as "The Principle of Relaxation and Neocatharsis") and an introduction of his later paper on the "Termination of the Analysis." In his stay in Baden-Baden, Ferenczi took seven of his patients with him, which shows both his conviction and dedication to the analysis he con-ducted, as well as how analyses were carried out at the time and that may be found very different from how they were later conducted in classical clinical settings. At the time, Ferenczi expressed his con-fidence and satisfaction with the clinical work he was conducting.

Groddeck also played an important role in the Freud and Ferenczi dispute since a part of their disagreements revolved around the attitude of indifference and mockery on the part of Freud towards Groddeck. Freud liked Groddeck personally, but had great doubts regarding his scientific potential for the psy-choanalytic movement. In December 1, 1925, Freud wrote to Ferenczi telling him that "Groddeck was here just at my worst time. I saw him only once for an hour. Personally, I like him very much, but scientifically, he is probably not usable; he overtaxed himself with the Ψ influence on the organic and [with] the It, and he is not the right man for working out that idea" (p. 238).

## Foreign pupils and Ferenczi's warm reception in America

In the 1920s, psychoanalysts in Europe began to have a large influx of foreign pupils. There was a growing interest from overseas analysands, which came to Europe for analysis with Freud and Ferenczi. Ferenczi and Freud wrote to each other about the importance that psychoanalysis was taking in France and in Sao Paulo, Brazil. I was also a time in which Ferenczi felt his health and his professional practice strengthened.

In May 25, 1924, Ferenczi mentioned to Freud that he had been invited to lecture in the United States: "[I] recently received an invitation from America, this time to participate in the founding and putting into operation of a psychoanalytic polyclinic, for which the money is supposedly available. I am supposed to stay there two or three years. This eventuality comes into consideration for me only as a financial one, since I would rather do my work on the continent. I responded evasively, and am awaiting Rank's information about America" (p. 151). In his initial letters to Freud, Ferenczi is hesitant about accepting the invitation. Eventually he will accept and it will prove to be of great value for him professionally and, as he expected, financially.

In 1924, Ferenczi published with Otto Rank the book *The Development of Psychoanalysis*. Though initially it was praised by Freud, it eventually triggered a series of conflicts within the Secret Committee. Rank's subsequent book, *The Trauma of Birth*, published that same year, was intensely criticized by Freud and marked Rank's final departure from the psychoanalytic movement. Other polemic issues around that time were Ferenczi's *Thalassa*, Reik and the problem of lay psychoanalysis and, later on, the conflicts between Anna Freud and Melanie Klein and the death of Karl Abraham (Gallardo, 1996). In *The Development of Psychoanalysis*, Ferenczi and Rank talked about "the reintroduction of techniques such as hypnosis and suggestion in analytic therapy to accelerate therapy" (Fazeder & Barant, 2000, pp. XXII and XXIII). Freud was reluctant to follow his approach and conclusions and furthermore thought that the innovations mentioned in the text were not without danger. The topic of Rank's book, his personal relationship with Freud and Ferenczi, and his alliance to the psychoanalytic movement are greatly discussed in the Freud-Ferenczi correspondence during the years 1924 and 1925.

Despite having lectured at Clark University in 1909, Freud was not fond of the American culture and criticized in many ways. He feared that psychoanalysis would become a servant of psychiatry and in retrospective it can be seen that his fears were not oversized (Fergusson, 2015, p. 99). In a letter to Ferenczi, Freud (1925) mentions that he "recently offended an American with the suggestion that the Statue of Liberty in New York harbour should be replaced by a monkey holding up a Bible" (Fazeder & Barant, 2000, p. 227). Ferenczi seems to have been more open, or have less antipathy, to America, and he was well greeted and successful in his lectures and analyses conducted in the United States. Ferenczi mentioned to Freud the possibility of staying a few months in Vienna as a first option or in the United States, but asked Freud for an opinion on which he thinks would be the best option, to which Freud replies that, if he wants to move to Vienna, his analysis doesn't have to be the motive. It is in *Letter 1060* that Ferenczi confirms his decision to travel to the United States since in Vienna it is difficult for him to find housing, whereas in the United States he "consolidates relationships and ensures his future" (p. 259). Ferenczi wrote to Freud about all the emotional and practical aspects of his trip to America. He also gave details about the lectures he was going to give, presenting to Freud his program of 18 conferences he would deliver in New York.

Also, the mater of lay analysis was a topic that interested Freud and Ferenczi deeply. On one side, the United States and European analysts argued that medical training was essential for anyone who wanted to treat patients. But, on the other side, the Hungarian group (which included Freud and Ferenczi), argued in favour of the training of non-physicians, as was supported by Freud's paper entitled "The Question of Lay Analysis." In the United States, it was a student of Brill who managed to elude the approval of a bill in New York that avoided non-physicians to train as analysts.

In the United States, Ferenczi was well received by the American analysts, and it was quickly seen how he has a great influence in the dissemination of Freud's publications in the United States. Ferenczi published a paper entitled "The Significance of Freud for Mental Hygiene." Regarding it, Freud stated that he was: "[v]ery pleased that you are letting us experience jointly everything that happens to you there" (p. 286). Ferenczi reminds Freud that he follows his injunction regarding "don't let yourself be strucked dry by the Americans" (p. 288). In the academic aspects, Ferenczi commented on the great influence and the great rise of John B. Watson (1878–1958), who also lectured at the *New School* on his advances on behaviourism. Regarding his theories, Ferenczi says that conditioned reflexes would be understood from the psycho-analytic perspective as a more complex psychic processes. He also talks about Adolf Meyer and his manuscript in which a "controlled anger over psychoanalysis" is evidenced (p. 293). Freud responds by telling him that he found in his letter the American touch char-acterized by the lack of details regarding Ferenczi's well-being. Nonetheless, their academic and personal relationship seems solid. Freud mentions frequently his health problems and annoyances regarding his prosthetic.

This trip to New York, that lasts almost a year, allowed Ferenczi to continue the analysis of former analysands living in the United States. He has the chance to meet H.S. Sullivan and, before re-turning to Budapest, went to London to meet Jones, as well as his analysand Melanie Klein, and later to Baden-Baden to spend the summer with Groddeck, and finally to Berlin to meet Eitington. His last stop was Vienna for his acquaintance with Freud, who seems to be upset that Ferenczi had not met him sooner after having arrived from America (Bokanowski, 1997, p. 24).

## Note

1  https://www.wapol.org/en/Template.asp

Chapter 7

# Thalassa and bioanalysis

Ferenczi produced two of the strangest books in the history of psychoanalysis. One of them, not intended for publication, was the *Clinical Diary* (1932), to which we will refer to further on, and the other one was *Thalassa. A Theory of Genitality*. Published in 1924, it is a bold insertion into what he names "bioanalysis." Taking into account E. H. A. Haeckel's work (a distinguished naturalist) and Jean-Baptiste Lamarck's evolutionary theories, Ferenczi links the history of evolution to the development of sexuality from child to adulthood. Freud (1933) mentions this project in Ferenczi's obituary and states that: "This little book is a biological rather than a psycho-analytic study; it is an application of the attitudes and insights associated with psycho-analysis to the biology of the sexual processes and, beyond them, to organic life in general. It was perhaps the boldest application of psycho-analysis that was ever attempted. It is probable that some time in the future there will really be a 'bio-analysis', as Ferenczi has prophesied" (p. 228).

Ferenczi began working on this book during WWI, in the Hungarian frontier, where he served as the doctor of a brigade of hussars. It will be only ten years later, and with Freud's frequent encouragement, that he would finally publish it. As he mentions in the introduction

> Gradually the conviction grew upon me that such an importation into psychology of concepts belonging to the

DOI: 10.4324/9780367854355-7

field of natural science, and into the natural sciences of psychological concepts, was inevitable and might be extremely fruitful [...] [A]ll physical and physiological phenomena require a metaphysical (i.e., psychological) explanation and all psychological phenomena a meta-psychological (i.e., physical) one. Emboldened by the acquisition of this insight and by the fact that the results at which I arrived with the aid of this method have found unexpected confirmation in the most recent and quite differently oriented investigations of others, I have decided upon the publication of the present volume. (Ferenczi, 1924, p. 3)

Ferenczi believes there is a primitive ego that is present in foetal life. In parallel to the transformation required in animals in their passing from the ocean to the land, the amphibious transformations for aerobic functioning, the born child must pass from the liquid foetal environment to the aerobic respiration, and that first inhaling of oxygen transforms it forever. Ferenczi states that in every human there persists a desire to return to intrauterine life. The coitus in the adult male is guided by an impulse to return to the mother's womb and to coming back to "Thalassa," the primordial sea and mother of all mothers.

In Ferenczi, we can find these original and keen thoughts regarding the articulation between the phylogenetic and the ontogenetic developments of the species in general and of humans in particular. He also emphasizes the importance of the inorganic, with a clear reference to Freud's conception of the death drive as an impulse to return to an inorganic state which preceded all life forms. In the case of Ferenczi, it corresponds to the repetition of a primitive catastrophe: that which led to the geological transformations of the planet, forcing the living organisms out of the primordial sea, which in humans is present in the catastrophe of leaving the maternal body, and that can only be partially and symbolically recovered through coitus and, eventually, death. In every human, Ferenczi argues, there is this tendency towards returning to that intrauterine existence: "In the light of this 'bioanalytic' conception of genital processes, as I should like to term it, it becomes comprehensible for the first time why the Oedipus wish, the wish for sexual intercourse with the mother, recurs so regularly, with an almost wearisome monotony, as the central striving in the analysis of the male. The Oedipus wish is precisely the psychological expression of an extremely general biological tendency which lures the organism to a return to the state of rest enjoyed before birth" (Ferenczi, 1924, p. 19). The prevalent hypothesis in this book is the existence of an intrauterine life that is a repetition of the phylogenetic development of the species, this regarding the marine origin of animal life. Every sexual act implies a transit through the vicissitudes of the species in its phylogenetic and ontogenetic history.

The coitus, which ends in the Ego's triumph of ejaculation, strives to conquer the female body, returning to the maternal womb, there were there was no differentiation between the Ego and the world. It evidences the Ego's compulsion to dissolve itself, to become no-Ego once again. The orgasm is not only the return to intrauterine tranquillity, but the equanimity of inorganic existence. Ferenczi believes that birth does not constitute a permanent traumatism. Instead, it is a passing event, that marks a discontinuity from uterine life, but that can be repaired if the infant is received by an adequate environment.

## Chapter 8

# The end of analysis

It could be stated that Ferenczi inaugurates a unique human desire: the desire to conduct a psychoanalysis to the end, to its final consequences, to the conclusion of the experience of the unconscious. Authors such as Wladimir Granoff (2004) and Yves Lugrin (2017) have stated that even though Freud is the undoubtable founding father of psychoanalysis, Ferenczi is the first true analyst. They see Ferenczi in a much more radical light than that in which he has been read by certain authors (such as Winnicott) and schools, and closer to how Michael Balint and Jacques Lacan have appreciated: Ferenczi as "the most pertinent of the first-generation authors to question what was required of an analyst, especially in regard to the end of treatment" (Lacan, 1955, cited by Lugrin, 2017).

In "The principle of relaxation and neocatharsis" (1931), Ferenczi states that "it is essential for the analyst himself to go through an analysis reaching to the very deepest depths and putting him into control of his own character-traits" (p. 124). Ferenczi promoted the analysis of the psychoanalyst: The lack of analysis of the analyst "can lead to the intolerable situation that our patients are better analysed than ourselves" (Ferenczi, 2012/1932e: 250; see also *Clinical Diary*, 1932c, p. 137) and the need to carry that analysis to the end.

In September 3, 1927, Ferenczi presented his paper entitled "On the problem of the termination of the analysis" in the tenth International Psycho-Analytical Congress which was held

DOI: 10.4324/9780367854355-8

in Innsbruck, Austria. In his lecture, Ferenczi begins by addressing a certain clinical difficulty: he has discovered that a patient that he has been treating for eight months has been lying to him regarding an important financial issue. By lying about this, the patient has failed to follow the basic psychoanalytic principle of communicating to the analyst his true and complete ideas and associations. Ferenczi had referred to this case in his correspondence with Freud. In August 3, 1926, Ferenczi wrote to his colleague: "I am writing this time to share with you a small discovery. In a patient who accomplished the feat of forgetting an entire day of his life (and in the process experienced all kinds of things, but mostly 'forbidden' ones on that day), who thus produced one of the otherwise so famous instances of splitting of the personality, I found out that this symptom was an indirect (and unconscious) communication in my direction, to wit, that he had consciously concealed from me or misrepresented to me a whole lot of things. I am convinced that all other instances of this kind can be explained in a similar way – they are an admission of *mendacity*, that is to say, the fact that, in various situations in their lives or in relation to various groups of people, these people expose only parts of their total character and conceal a large part of their behaviour. The cause lies, naturally, in the infantile lie in sexual matters – at the same time, an imitation of the mendacity of adults" (p. 272).

Continuing with his presentation regarding the end of analysis, Ferenczi asks, what is the analyst to do if the pathological aspect of the patient is precisely lying? Ferenczi questions if a patient's mendacity would imply a limit to the psychoanalytic technique, but he refuses to accept this lightly. He refers to a former incident with this patient in which he misses one of his sessions and, the day after, makes no mention of his omission. When interrogated by the analyst about this, the patient initially refuses to accept that he has missed his session and only afterwards does he recognize that he has missed it, but has no memory of what he did instead. Through the testimonies of other people, the patient is able to reconstruct the events, in which he has spent the day in a state of semi-drunkenness with people stranger to him and of ill reputation. Ferenczi concluded that the patient's split personality is a sign of the neurotic mendacity of the patient and an evidence of a defect in his character. Therefore, at least in this case, he states, the patient's lying was favourable for the analysis for it allowed revealing this aspect of the patient's neurotic functioning. Addressing the issues of lying and simulation in neurosis and hysteria, Ferenczi states that: "A real abandonment of mendacity therefore appears to be at least a sign of the approaching end of the analysis" (p. 78).

What is referred to as lies in the adult are in relation to what are mentioned as fantasies in the child. One of the main directions of the cure in cases of hysteria has been the unveiling of the fantasies that constitute the patient's psychic reality[1]. But Ferenczi believes it is necessary to reconstruct the patient's reality, differentiating it from the fantasies associated to it. It would require the patient to abandon his tendency to, for example, omit certain events or associations in order to preserve a good image of himself onto the analyst. The paradox which Ferenczi humorously mentions is that the fundamental rule of psychoanalysis can only be fully achieved once the analysis has ended.

Infantile lying, which is used to avoid a perceived greater displeasure as a consequence of honesty, underlies the future development of morality. The passage from a state of amorality to one of morality requires the renunciation to the satisfaction of certain drives. This renunciation and acceptance of certain discontents, speculates Ferenczi, is most probably perceived by the child initially with a feeling of untruth, as a hypocritical act. The analysis most go as deep as to the instinctual foundations that lead to a certain character formation, giving rise to a new and better personality. In this sense, the end of analysis must go beyond a symptom analysis, into a character analysis.

Ferenczi mentions important effects of a completed analysis in a subject. Due to having achieved a separation between his fantasies and reality, the analysed person has "an almost unlimited inner freedom and simultaneously a much surer grip in acting and making decisions" (p. 81). Following this, he refers to the fact that, in many cases, cured neurotics preserve *tics* and mannerisms despite the resolution of their symptoms and believes that a character analysis must address this issues and, in a sense, put a mirror on the patient's face so he can, for the first time, see his oddities and strangeness of his functioning and even of his physical appearance. This is not directly mentioned by the analyst to the patient, but it is the patient who must become aware of it with the help of the analyst. With this, Ferenczi shows his interest in psychoanalysis not only touching the patient's psyche, but also his body. This idea of the effect of analysis in the body is what has been more thoroughly developed in his work on "bioanalysis" referred to in the previous chapter.

Ferenczi refers to the factor of time and believes that analysis requires having indefinite time available: the more unlimited, the greater the chance for success. But he wisely specifies that more than the time at his disposal, it is the patient's disposition to carry out his analysis with the determination to persist as long as it is necessary. He mentions that abruptly ending an analysis could produce an effect in certain cases, but believes it cannot be recommended as a valid technique, in what appears to be a clear reference (and a distance) from Freud's analysis of Sergei Pankejeff (known as the "Wolf Man"). In an analysis, the whole array of the patient's memories, repetitions and "working through" are displayed. Transference (though not named with that term) and the overall patient-analyst relation is crucial; on the side of the patient, regarding his dependence and mistrust of the analyst, and on the side of the analyst, the importance of sincerity, of recognizing his mistakes and not responding to the patient's attitude from his own intrinsic, unresolved, dispositions. This is why Ferenczi insists in the need for the analyst to be completely analysed. Ferenczi mentions that he does not find structural differences between "so-called" training analysis and therapeutic analysis. He believes it is not enough with a one year analysis for the analyst: he has to have undertaken a complete analysis of his unconscious.

"The proper ending of an analysis," says Ferenczi, "is when neither the physician nor the patient puts an end to it, but when it dies of exhaustion, so to speak" (p. 85). We will go back to this assertion. Regarding the transference with the analyst, it falls as well at the end of analysis: "A truly cured patient frees himself from analysis slowly but surely" (p. 85). Later, in his *Clinical Diary*

(1932), Ferenczi mentions that the end of analysis implies the emancipation of the patient from the analyst. Ferenczi also mentions that it is common to find symptom transformations towards the end of analysis; for example, a hysteric presenting obsessive ideas, conversion symptoms in obsessional intellectuality, and even temporary psychosis in neurotic patients.

In this ground-breaking paper, Ferenczi present ideas regarding the ending of analysis that are pertinent for present times. He believes that analysis are not interminable, that there is a logical end to them and that many times the causes of analysis not reaching and end lie in the insufficient analysis of the analyst and his incapacity to see and recognize the weak points of his personality.

Going back to his remark according to which "The proper ending of an analysis is when neither the physician nor the patient puts an end to it, but when it dies of exhaustion, so to speak" (p. 85), it is worth highlighting that the German term that Ferenczi uses for termination is *Erschöpfung*. Its etymology is the noun of the verb *erschöpfen* (and this, in turn, is a derivation of *"er"* + *"schöpfen."* *Schöpfen* can be used as taking out (a liquid) or taking (air). Because of this, with the prefix *"er"* it implies taking out or removing completely, that is, "exhausting." Therefore, "exhaustion" is a correct translation of the word, but it is worth specifying its polyvalence, beyond its common use as a state of severe fatigue. *Erschöpfung* refers to "exhaustion" also in the sense of exhausting completely an existing source, for example, exhausting the natural resources present in a certain source, such as the precious rocks available in a mine. Once the resources have been extracted completely, there is nothing else to retrieve from that source. Ferenczi makes it clear that what is "exhausted" is not the analyst or the analysand, but the analysis itself. It is the moment when the experience of the unconscious is terminated and, we can say, when there is no more unconscious material available for extraction.

But *Erschöpfung* allows an even deeper level of analysis. The word *Schöpfen*, present in *Erschöpfung*, refers to a creation, in the sense of an artistic, very formal creation. *Schöpfen* is also the creator, as in the "Creator of all things," or as in the Creator (*Schöpfer*) and the creature/created (*Geschöpf*). In a very ceremonial sense, one would also speak of an artist as a creator (*Schöpfer*), implying the creation of something very original. In this sense, what can be found at the end of an analysis, in the termination of its experience, is not only the exhaustion of the experience of the unconscious, but an absolutely original creation on behalf of the subject. This creation is not something that is elaborated *ex Nihilo* or "out of the blue," but precisely a remnant once the reduction of the unconscious through the analysis has isolated that singular formation of the subject that can allow him to engage in a new relation with his reality and with his own psyche. This is different from Freud's understanding of the end of analysis, present in his "Terminable and Interminable Analysis" (1937), and much closer to Lacan's later elaborations regarding analysis as the isolation of the incurable dimension of the subject and of the concept of "sinthome" as that element that is rediscovered in the end of analysis, which is linked intimately to the subject's singularity, being a consequence of his unconscious decisions anand complexity, is worth transcribingd desires and of his historical contingencies, and that, through the experience of his analysis, he can transform from a source of suffering to an authentic form of enjoyment (*jouissance*), which becomes the key mark of the subject's relation with his existence.

## The analysis of the psychoanalyst

In many occasions Ferenczi insists in the importance of the analysis of the analyst (Fergusson, 2015a, p. 192). The three main pillars of psychoanalytic training (psychoanalysis of the analyst, clinical supervision and study of the psychoanalytic theories and doctrine) are a Ferenczian contribution that still exists today and that are a common ground in all psychoanalytic associations and schools, despite the important differences present amongst them. As he writes in "Confusion of tongues between the adult and the child" (1933): "This leads to the side issue—the analysis of the analyst—which is becoming more and more important. Do not let us forget that the deep-reaching analysis of a neurosis needs many years, while the average training analysis lasts only a few months, or at most, one to one and a half years. This may lead to an impossible situation, namely, that our patients gradually become better analysed than we ourselves are, which means that although they may show signs of such superiority, they are unable to express it in words; indeed, they deteriorate into an extreme submissiveness obviously because of this inability or because of a fear of occasioning displeasure in us by their criticism" (p. 158).

Ferenczi also believed that psychoanalysis had a power to awaken people and that, in that sense, it proceeded in a direction contrary to hypnosis. If hypnosis refers to the effect of language producing an order from an other, order that is unconscious for the subject, psychoanalysis points towards awakening the subject to those orders of the other which he has confused with his own will and which he fulfils with his actions, not knowing that it is the will of an other that he is fulfilling through those acts.

In 1924, Ferenczi wrote a very impressive letter that, due to its richness and complexity, is worth transcribing completely. The communication is directed to Frédéric Karinthy (1887–1938), a journalist of his time who initially was quite fond of psychoanalysis, but who afterwards loses interest in it. Ferenczi writes:

> My dear Karinthy ... You said that you knew two types of wise man and two types of science. The first [type of science] searches for the truth and strives to awaken a sleepy humanity; the second one avoids by all means disturbing the quietude of the drowsy world and even tends to make it fall into a deeper slumber. Psychoanalysis, you said, possesses that special ability to awaken us, trying to give the human psyche, by means of knowledge, not only command over oneself but also of our organic and physical strengths.
>
> But now you write that it is necessary to stop being in [psycho-] analysis in order to preferably study those who speak of peace, harmony, welfare, and that, with the help of clever suggestions, including hypnotic dreams, surreptitiously introduce in the human psyche sensations, ideas and reasonable, intelligent, comforting and joyful intentions.
>
> I have previously found your words regarding the power of the wise somewhat audacious, but since then I have been able to convince myself of their certainty. I recognized in principle the ability of "awakener" which corresponded to

psychoanalysis and I have not changed my mind, because I am convinced that without an authentic and brave science, any effort to find happiness is useless and at best can only arouse a temporary illusion. But you, on the contrary, have apparently lost patience (possibly due to present miseries); you neither wish the truth nor science and only aspire to find a bit of joy for our tormented world at any price, even if it means lulling it to sleep. In a word, I would simply wish to acknowledge here that, of us two, I am now the one who has not abandoned the ranks of those who awaken.

There is a difference, for Ferenczi between a science that "lulls" and a science that "awakens." This awakening power of psychoanalysis was present in his first readings of psychoanalysis and prevailed throughout his work. This was what he believed to be the true power of psychoanalysis and what gave it is potentially to change not only the individual's psychic suffering, but to change society itself. If the analysts are the ones carrying out these fundamental processes, the need for them to carry out their own analysis to its end is certainly much more imperative. It is a Ferenczian legacy that the ethics of the analyst implies not retreating in his desire delve as deep as he can into his own unconscious.

## Note

1 This inevitably evokes Lacan's proposal of the end of analysis as a "traversée du fansasme."

# Chapter 9

# Ferenczi's interest in the psychology of the child: upbringing and education

Throughout his work, Ferenczi makes explicit his interest in what psychoanalysis can contribute to the matters of education and of upbringing. He is aware that psychoanalysis is suspicious of giving advice, but believes it can shed light, more than in how to raise children, in how not to raise them. In his lecture, "The adaptation of the family to the child" (1927), he inverts the common conception that it is the child who should adapt to his family and to his environment. Instead, Ferenczi believes that it is the family that should become aware of the psychic processes of the child and be of aid to him to help him understand what he feels and needs. Ferenczi criticizes the adult hypocrisy in presenting themselves to the child as immaculate and idealized figures, whose bodies and mind function perfectly and are devoid of sexual impulses.

He mentions certain "traumata," as he names them, which can be especially intense for the child, such as "weaning," toilet training and sexual and egoistic impulses, much more than birth itself. These early events in the life of a child, says Ferenczi, can have great impact in the rest of his life: "Just as, if you have only one candle in a room and put your hand near the candle, half the room may become darkened, so if, near the beginning of life, you do only a little harm to a child, it may cast a shadow over the whole of its life" (Ferenczi, 1927, p. 65). In this paper, Ferenczi states that the child tends to love that which he believes to be a part of him, including his excrements: "his excreta are really part of himself, a transitional something between him and his

DOI: 10.4324/9780367854355-9

environment, i.e., between subject and object" (Ferenczi, 1927, p. 67). The function of certain objects as "transitional" for the child will be an idea further developed by Donald W. Winnicott, as well as that of the importance of the environment and the conceptualisations on the true and false selves, though with minimal references to the work of Ferenczi, which constitutes a clear antecedent of his theoretical and technical developments (for the relation between the work of Ferenczi and Winnicott, see: Gutiérrez-Peláez & Herrera-Pardo, 2017). In this paper, he also refers to the importance of symbols in children, and idea that Melanie Klein (who was present when he presented the lecture and inquired on this matter) will develop in psychoanalysis.

Also, Ferenczi finds that most frequently teachers and parents often want to remove what they believe to be abnormal in the child. On the contrary, he believes that they should not be "downhearted about [these abnormal dispositions], for these primitive functions provide us with energy for the great achievements of civilization. [...] Teachers often wish to 'weed out' these primitive urges (which are most important sources of energy) as if they were vices, whereas if led into social channels they can be used for the good of the individual and for the benefit of society" (Ferenczi, 1927, p. 69). It is thanks to these dispositions, to their sublimation, and not despite of them, that humans are able to contribute to culture and civilization and establish possible social bonds amongst them. He encourages teachers and parents to not be too afraid of the word "masturbation" and the manifestation of this conduct in the child. Being open and understanding of the child's impulses can lead to the development of a less cruel and severe Super-Ego, alleviating the child in puberty and adulthood from the suffering it can exert over him.

In "Child Analysis in the Analysis of Adults" (1931), Ferenczi states that: "I have had a kind of fanatical belief in the efficacy of depth-psychology, and this has led me to attribute occasional failures not so much to the patient's 'incurability' as to our own lack of skill, a supposition which necessarily led me to try altering the usual technique in severe cases with which it proved unable to cope successfully" (p. 128). Here, Ferenczi refers both to the importance of taking the analysis of the analyst to the end, as well as the need to introduce changes in the technique to favour the progress in the treatment of certain patients. He then continues: "It is thus only with the utmost reluctance that I ever bring myself to give up even the most obstinate case, and I have come to be a specialist in peculiarly difficult cases, with which I go on for very many years. I have refused to accept such verdicts as that a patient's resistance was unconquerable, or that his narcissism prevented our penetrating any further, or the sheer fatalistic acquiescence in the so-called 'drying up' of a case. I have told myself that, as long as a patient continues to come at all, the last thread of hope has not snapped. Thus the question constantly forced itself upon me: Is it always the patient's resistance that is the cause of the failure? Is it not rather our own convenience, which disdains to adapt itself, even in technique, to the idiosyncrasies of the individual?" (p. 128). This approach towards the treatment and cure of the patients, even those regarded as the most difficult, shows Ferenczi's strong belief in the possibilities of psychoanalysis.

In his paper "The Unwelcome Child and its Death Instinct" (1929), Ferenczi refers to those children that are "unwelcome guest" to a home that has no place for them. The effects of a mother than has not opened in her desire a place for these children, with "aversion or impatience on the part of the mother," weakens in them their will to live and unleashes, so to speak, the most morbid aspects of their death drives. But also, the "life force" requires an environment that allows it to develop and to strengthen sufficiently in order to face de harsh struggles present in every living being's existence. Ferenczi also mentions the importance of looking into the psychological differences in children that have been "maltreated from the start," from "those who are at first received with enthusiasm, indeed with passionate love, but then 'dropped'" (Ferenczi, 1929, p. 106). We can see this theoretical and clinical elaborations in Ferenczi as a clear antecedent of the differences between "privation" and "deprivation" which will have their importance in the theoretical developments of the British school of psychoanalysis.

To conclude this chapter, it is worth mentioning that Ferenczi also wrote about the clinical treatment of children. One of his most iconic papers is that of the case of Arpad[1], which more than one of his patients was close to him socially, even though he was able to see him in his consultation room. The particularity of Arpad, a five-year-old boy, was his both fear and fascination with domesticated birds. Arpad burst in great excitement in his visits to the fowl-house, imitated the birds movements and sounds, both their habitual crow and crackle, as well as their noises of agony when being sacrificed for human consumption. Ferenczi links Arpad's mental functioning to a fear of castration for onanism. This case report is one of the earliest published psychoanalytic papers in what we could locate today in the spectrum of child psychoses.

## Note

1 Published under the name "A Little Chanticleer" in the *International Zeitschrift* in 1913.

## Chapter 10

# Ferenczi's latest writings. The effect of "confusion of tongues" and his *Clinical Diary*

In Freud's and Ferenczi's correspondence between 1927 and 1929, a growing tension can be perceived between the two psychoanalysts. There are conflicts between Ferenczi and Ernest Jones, who appears to be an obstacle for Ferenczi's presidency of the IPA. Ferenczi decided not to run due to the existing differences regarding secular analysis. Eitingon, who was also interested in the presidency, was reluctant to hand it over to Ferenczi, also related to the disagreements on the matter of lay analysts. Freud, who had the same position as Ferenczi regarding this issue, wrote to Ferenczi with gratitude for his introduction to the book on "Lay Analysis" and said that: "Since 1909 we have covered a nice piece of trail with each other, always hand in hand, and it won't be any different for the short stretch that still remains to be trod" (p. 327). To his letter, Ferenczi replies by saying: "The thanks that we owe you for the light that you brought to the darkness of knowledge about man" (p. 328) and emphasizes that their friendship began long before (1907) the year mentioned by Freud.

In January 1, 1928, Ferenczi sends Freud his manuscript "The Elasticity of the Psycho-analytical Technique," "requesting his opinion on the paper all together" (p. 331). Freud highlights Ferenczi's maturity saying that "your enclosed paper – here re-inclosed – testifies to that superior maturity that you have acquired in the last few years and in which no one approaches you" (p. 332). He criticizes Ferenczi's concept of "tact," finding it the most questionable element in his paper, as it can be subjective

DOI: 10.4324/9780367854355-10

and has a "mystical character for beginners" (p. 332). Ferenczi refutes this criticism, stating that it is not subjective in the sense that it only affirms that it should be put in the position of the patient and "empathize [*einfühlen*]" (p. 334), a feeling that should be located in the preconscious and not in the unconscious. During this time, Ferenczi was in a great professional conditions. He gave lectures in the Hungarian Psychoanalytic Society, which he directed since 1913, and psychoanalysts from different countries attended his conferences (as the case of Wilhelm Reich).

## Ferenczi's lectures and influence in Spain

Ferenczi was invited to Spain to give lectures between September and November of 1928. In Madrid, he meet Dr. José María Sacristan, the director of the asylum, and later Dr. Ballesteros, who asked him to give a conference to a select group of intellectuals on "the training of the psychoanalyst and the focus on the analyst's being analysed." Ferenczi mentioned to Freud that it has been an interesting group and of the highest nobility, led by the Duchess of Alba. The influence of Ferenczi can be highlighted for its role in the rise of the psychoanalytic movement in Europe.

After this meeting, Ferenczi received a letter from Luis Lopez Ballesteros in which he thanked him for the impulse he gave him to fight for the psychoanalytic movement, saying that

> Since I have not yet been granted the pleasure of knowing the father of psychoanalysis personally, I was very fortunate to honour him in the person of one of his most loyal and more sage adherents. Dr. Ferenczi, with his forceful, youthful spirit, has instilled in me the courage to continue, or perhaps better said, to begin, the fight for psychoanalysis here. (p. 353)

Lopez Ballesteros was one of the translators of Freud's works to Spanish. With time, Freud's and Ferenczi's letters become more distant and less affectionate. There are increasing tensions in the psychoanalytic movement due to the enmity of Ferenczi with Ernest Jones. Ferenczi sees in Jones an unscrupulous man.

Freud tells Ferenczi that on Anna Freud's opinion, he is isolating himself, and considers she has an important role as an intermediary to "solve this little, quite superfluous disturbance" (p. 381). On the other hand, Freud also tells him that he has the personal impression that although the IPA focuses on Berlin, Vienna and Budapest, only the first two have close relationships and leave Budapest isolated.

The distance between Freud and Ferenczi becomes more evident towards the end of the correspondence. This detachment took place due to the contrary ideas on the part of these two psychoanalysts about whether the new findings made by Ferenczi were contradictory to psychoanalysis. Ferenczi was determined in his ideas, as Freud grew increasingly skeptical of the therapeutic potential of psychoanalysis. At this time, there is also an enthusiasm and persistence on the part of Freud to make Ferenczi run for the presidency, but Ferenczi refused his candidacy.

Nonetheless these discrepancies, certain letters manage to present their creativity and search for progress in the psychoanalytic theory and technique. Ferenczi and Freud discussed Ferenczi's idea of "Traumatic fragmentation" (p. XXXIII), to which Freud agreed with much of the theory, but not with the term "scar formation" (p. XXXIII), since he argued that pathological psychological reactions related to trauma are less rigid than a scar. Ferenczi takes up the conversation saying that he wants the correspondence to return to its old path and that he would like to avoid unpleasant feelings and not for doubts about him to arise in Freud. He concludes that only frankness and honesty can help. A few letters after, Ferenczi expresses joy for reading the word "friend" in Freud's letter. This conflict, in its beginning apparently constituted of small discrepancies, will eventually increase and lead to irreversible misunderstandings between the two analysts.

Regarding the tensions between them, Ferenczi says that he is divided into various feelings and attitudes, since Freud was his revered teacher and unattainable model and later became his analyst (although he could not analyse him completely). Freud comments on all this by saying that he is confident that this bad feeling between them will not last long. Ferenczi responds to this by saying that it was not easy for him to see how a malaise could arise between them.

Their communications, despite the protagonist role of their relationship, continues to deal nonetheless with academic issues. For example, they talk about Ferenczi's impression about Freud's book "Civilization and Its Discontents" (1930), expressing he finds it lucid and admirable. As for the personal, Freud appreciates the reception given by Ferenczi to his daughter Anna. After this, both friends meet personally and express their happiness of being healthy and feeling like family.

Linked to this, Ferenczi tells Freud that: "I left [your house] with the conviction that my fear that my somewhat too independent manner of working and thinking could bring me into such painful conflict with you was exaggerated to high degree" (p. 392). Freud comments that Ferenczi's new ideas about the fragmentation of mental life seem ingenious to him and that they somewhat resemble the theory of genitality. Faced with the latter, Ferenczi comments that, although he thanks him for saying that they are "ingenious," he would have preferred "correct or plausible" and that his relationship with the theory of genitality is only superficial. Related to the theoretical aspects, Ferenczi also talks about the concept of "scar formation" (p. 400), on which he comments that "I find that the expression 'scar formation', as far as my experience goes, does not characterize mastery of trauma by means of pathological reaction quite accurately, inasmuch as the mental pathological products are not so rigid and incapable of regeneration as are the scars of bodily tissues" (p. 400). Ferenczi is interested in his research on traumatogenesis. He is also working on the project of the translation of Freud's works into Hungarian.

Despite these growing tensions, the Freud–Ferenczi relationship's catastrophic outcome came to its peak as a result of Ferenczi's writing, "Confusion of languages between the adult and the child" (1984/1932a and 2012/1932e). By the time, Ferenczi was 59 and Freud 76 years old. Freud reproached Ferenczi for returning to his first traumatic theory, which he thought of as a matter that the psychoanalytic theory had overcome. This was in fact the reading made by later generations of analysts, some to criticize this fact, some to exalt it. But, in fact, Ferenczi was not returning to a first Freudian seduction theory, but was instead introducing novel clinical, epistemic and practical ideas that over the years have found their rightful place in contemporary psychoanalysis (Gutiérrez-Peláez, 2009).

Freud had a negative reaction to the presentation of Ferenczi's paper "Confusion of tongues between adults and the child" (1932a). The paper was presented as the opening contribution at the XIIth Congress of Psychoanalysis, held in Wiesbaden, Germany, on 12 September 1932. Freud did not attend, apparently due to bad health, but he knew the paper for Ferenczi had read it to him some months before. According to Dupont (1985), "It was a painful encounter, in which mutual incomprehension between the two men came to a head. Freud, deeply shocked by the contents of the paper, demanded that Ferenczi refrain from publishing anything until he had reconsidered the position he put forth in it" (1985, pp. xvi–xvii). Freud tried to persuade Ferenczi from reading it.

Even though Freud did not attend, several analysts were present in Ferenczi's conference. Amongst them: "Anna Freud, Federn, Alexander, Jekels, Jones, de Groot, Brunswick, Simmel, Harnick, Bonaparte, Sterba, Reik, Balint, Deutsch, Rado, Weiss, Odier, Glover, Roheim, Menninger [and] de Saussure" (Masson, 1984, p. 151). The rejection of the paper was generalized amongst them, apparently most due to the fact that it was interpreted as a return to Freudian seduction theory, which had been "overcome" since the beginning of the century. Before 1897, Freud had developed a theory of the aetiology of neurosis that included hereditary factors, concomitant circumstances and specific causes, among these last being active seductions of infants by adults. Even though he abandons this theory by the early 1900s (in his *Letter 69* to his friend and colleague Wilhelm Fliess: "I do not believe in my neurotic"), there are other references in his later work that seem to revive it, as is the case of the "Wolf Man" and the analysis of the autobiography of Paul Schreber. These Freudian returns to the seduction theory throughout his work have led researchers to believe that there could be another cause of theoretical dispute in their conceptualizations regarding the death drive: "whereas for Freud there is a deadly component in every subject, for Ferenczi this component is attributable to the 'other'; it comes about owing to the traumatic effect of the other's action, and if this were not the case there would, in his view, be no reason for it to be unleashed" (Gutiérrez-Peláez, 2008). Ferenczi had referred to this aspect of the death drive before (Ferenczi, 1928 & 1929), explaining that the action of the other overflows the death drive, exceeding the capacity of the child's psyche to register and make of the traumatic event an experience. For Freud, on the other hand, the death drive is structural and operates always in the human psyche, though ideally embedded and to the service of the life drives.

Another complex episode that evolved in their letters has to do with the *Kusstechnick*. It seems that one of Ferenczi's patients, Clara Thompson[1], was saying in social circles that Ferenczi allowed her to kiss him. Freud wrote to Ferenczi telling him that he "made no secret of the fact that you kiss your patients and let them kiss you; I have also heard of the same thing from one of my patients" (p. 422). Freud sees a danger in this and what it could lead to in different analysts, stating that: "there is no revolutionary who is not knocked out of the field by still more radical one" (p. 422), as well as the critics towards psychoanalysis that it could arise.

Clara Thompson is referred to in Ferenczi's *Clinical Diary* (1932) as "Dm." In one of his entries, he mentions this issue

> Dm., a lady who, "complying" with my passivity had allowed herself to take more and more liberties, and occasionally even kissed me. Since this behaviour met with no resistances, since it was treated as something permissible in analysis and at most commented on theoretically, she remarked quite casually in the company of other patients, who were undergoing analysis elsewhere: "I am allowed to kiss Papa Ferenczi, as often as I like." (p. 423, footnote correspondence)

There is no evidence that this was a procedure that Ferenczi regularly applied, but instead seems to be an incident referred specifically to the case of this patient. Ferenczi replied to Freud's letter by saying that their disagreements are mixing in their relationship and that the "dishonourable" statement is incorrect, as well as Freud's fear that he will become another Stekel, but reassures him, as always, he will keep in mind the warnings he reproaches him and the effort to criticize him harshly. Finally, regarding this conflict, he says that he hopes their friendship will be re-established.

Another important issue at the time that was producing anxiety in the psychoanalytic movement was the possible bankruptcy of the *Verlag*. With its new director, Martin Freud, they decided to consult other members of the society, such as Lajos Levi, who could help financially for its maintenance. The importance of the publishing house and the journals are for them indisputable.

Freud reproaches Ferenczi for his negligence in the affairs of the association to what Ferenczi responds that he is right and that the cause is isolation due to his cases and also because he feels that he must go through periods of isolation in this late moment of his life. He believes that he had never allowed himself to rest psychically, which is why he is now experiencing a "super-exhaustion that lasts half a life" (p. 432).

In 1932 (though published in 1933), in a lecture entitled "Explanations, Applications and Orientations," Freud refers to a clinical example which we can clearly link to Ferenczi's case

> The therapeutic ambition of some of my adherents has made the greatest efforts to overcome these obstacles so that every sort of neurotic disorder might be curable by psycho-analysis. They have endeavoured to compress the work of analysis into a shorter duration, to intensify transference so that it may be able to overcome any resistance, to unite other forms of influence with it so as to compel a cure. These efforts are certainly praiseworthy, but, in my opinion, they are vain. They bring with them, too, a danger of being oneself forced away from analysis and drawn into a boundless course of experimentation. (Strachey, 1964, p. 140)

It is quite similar to the example he gives in his 1937 article "Terminable and interminable analysis," which in a sense constitutes a posthumous dialogue with his former analysand and pupil. Ferenczi informs Freud that, with all this in mind, he is not prepared for the presidency of the IPA. Freud responds by saying that he would like to insist on the presidency, but Ferenczi goes on to say that he cannot conceive the presidency since he does not even understand the full spectrum of his illness. Freud says he regrets this and that he does not make any sense of his arguments. Ferenczi tells Freud that he is not planning on taking distance from Freud or the psychoanalytic movement, saying that he feels "free of the tendency to found a new school."

After the meeting in which he read to Freud his paper "Confusion of tongues...," he wrote to Freud about his surprise regarding his advice to refrain from publishing or presenting the paper. Freud replies harshly by saying: "For three years you have been systematically turning away from me, probably developed a personal hostility that goes further than it could express itself ... I think I would be in a position to point out to you the theoretical error in your construction, but for what? I am convinced you would not be accessible to any doubts. So there is nothing left for me but to wish you the best, which would be very different from what is going on at present" (p. 445). This is the final breakup of their friendship and, in the stake of Ferenczi's impending death, there will be no time to amend it.

The two psychoanalysts begin the year 1933 by sharing two short notes. Ferenczi writes saying that he will "remain always conscious of the many years of being in good terms between us and of gratitude for your years of interest and kindness" (p. 446). Freud replies that, for him, it was not only being in good terms, "I think it was more than that, rather an intimate community of life, feeling, and interest" (p. 446).

After a couple of months, Ferenczi decides to interrupt his silence, to which he refers to as a "childish sulking" (p. 447) due to two factors: (1) the relapse of the pernicious anaemia and (2) his advice that Freud and Anna travel to England due to the rise of Nazis to power in Germany. In this letter, it is important to add that his handwriting overlaps and has errors, which is very uncharacteristic of him, and probably caused by his state of health "your handwriting really shows how tired you still are" (Freud, p. 448–449). Freud asks him to rest since his writing shows how affected he is and that his discussion on technical and theoretical matters can wait since for it is more important for him to regain his health. Finally, regarding his travel advice, he says he has not considered it and that it appears that the Hitler regime will now dominate Austria. There are many frequent mentions to the political convulsions of Europe at the time.

In May 4, 1933, Ferenczi writes his last letter to Freud: "Dear Professor, only a few lines to indicate to you that the date of your birthday is still in our memory. Let us hope that the year to come won't bring the same ugly events of the past. I am pretty much on an even keel; my symptoms are unchanged. I exert myself in giving credence to the optimistic statements of my doctors" (Falsberder & Barant, 2000, p. 450). Gizella, Ferenczi's wife, writes a note on the back of the paper informing Freud that Ferenczi is ill ("he is still not the one he was"), but that his doctor is optimistic of his recovery. She also wishes Freud her best for his birthday. Ferenczi will die a few days later of a pernicious anaemia.

As Freud (1933) will mention on Ferenczi's obituary, "our friend slowly drifted away from us. On his return from a period of work in America he seemed to withdraw more and more into solitary work, though he had previously taken the liveliest share in all that happened in analytic circles. We learnt that one single problem had monopolized his interest. The need to cure and to help had become paramount in him. He had probably set himself aims which, with our therapeutic means, are altogether out of reach to-day" (p. 229). We will refer to his death and reactions to in in the following chapters.

## Note

1 As stated in the footnote of the Freud-Ferenczi correspondence, "Clara Mabel Thompson (1893-1958), American analyst, can be viewed as the most influential pupil of and successor to Ferenczi in North America, by virtue of her general orientation and especially her works on countertransference and the personality of the analyst. At the urging of Harry Stack Sullivan, she was in analysis with Ferenczi in the summers of 1928 and 1929, and then continuously from 1931 until the latter's death. Along with Fromm and Sullivan, she founded the William A. White Institute in New York and the Washington School of Psychiatry" (p. 423).

# Chapter 11

# Ferenczi's trauma theory

In the last years of his life and career, Ferenczi wrote and produced abundant material on the theory of trauma and on therapeutic practice in relation to trauma. Dupont (1998) wrote that "Ferenczi constructed his theory of trauma [...] gradually, on the basis of clinical observations" (p. 236). It was Mikhail Balint who edited the compilation of his latest writings, entitled "Final Contributions to the Problems and Methods of Psychoanalysis" (Ferenczi, 1955). These works differ from his earlier works on the issue of trauma and in his overall understanding of the psychoanalytical practice and technique.

In Ferenczi's latest writings, there is a distance from Freud's ideas and they constitute an original contribution to psychoanalysis which continues to be most relevant and pertinent today. These latest works have raised diverse reactions in the psychoanalytic community, initially with intense criticism and rejection, and more recently with interest and praise. Ferenczi's *Clinical Diary* (1933) and his "Notes and fragments" (1930–32) illustrate his developing ideas on trauma and the psychic mechanisms involved in it, rather than presenting finished theories. As he presents it in his writings, trauma is referred to as an event that occurs within the adult–child relationship and has a direct effect on the development of the subject's narcissism.

In the paper "Confusion of tongues between adults and the child " (1932a), Ferenczi emphasises once again the external origin of trauma and its effects on the development of character

DOI: 10.4324/9780367854355-11

and psychoneurosis, highlighting the traumatic factor, which he believes has been minimised in psychoanalytic theory. Maybe this point is what has led to commentators and interpreters of Ferenczi's work to believe that he was mainly returning to earlier Freudian formulations and to overlook the original contribution contained within these writings.

In "Confusion of Tongues...", Ferenczi distinguishes two kinds of love: the child's tender love and the adult's erotic current. It is the adult's abusive confusion of both tongues that leads him to psychically, affectively and biologically pervade the child (what we could call an "adulterating adult"). The child, paralysed by intense fear, is defenceless against the adult's sexual assault. As stated by Ferenczi: "The same anxiety, however, if it reaches a certain maximum, compels them to subordinate themselves like automata to the will of the aggressor, to divide each one of his desires and to gratify these; completely oblivious of themselves they identify themselves with the aggressor. Through the identification, or let us say, introjection of the aggressor, he disappears as part of the external reality, and becomes intra- instead of extra-psychic; [...] the attack as a rigid external reality ceases to exist and in the traumatic trance the child succeeds in maintaining the previous situation of tenderness (Ferenczi, 1932a, p. 162). The concept of "identification with the aggressor" is a key concept of Ferenczi's traumatic theory. It is a shocking omission by Anna Freud to use this concept as a notion of her own, without citing Ferenczi.

An immediate effect is that the child introjects the adult's sense of guilt; this means that the adult's sexual intrusion is now transformed into something for which the child deserves to be punished. The child's apparent recovery is the evidence of his psychological splitting, being at the same time guilty and in-nocent, and disconnecting his relation to his own feelings, per-ceptions and sensations. A confusional state reigns the child's psychic activity. Paradoxically, more than defending himself, the child proceeds to identify with the aggressor and introjects what he perceives as a threat to him. This is what leads to the splitting of his personality. A part of his psyche registers the experience and other lives as if nothing has happened. As he expressed it in "Child-analysis in the analysis of adults": "It really seems as though, under the stress of imminent danger, part of the self splits off and becomes a psychic instance observing and desiring to help the self, and that possibly this happens in early – even the very earliest – childhood" (Ferenczi, 1931a, p. 136). A few lines before, in this article, he mentions: "One definitely gets the impression that to be left deserted results in a split of personality. Part of the person adopts the role of father or mother in relation to the rest, thereby undoing, as it were, the fact of being left deserted [...] [T]he 'narcissistic split of the self'" (p. 135).

In order to elaborate the trauma in the psychoanalytic treatment, the material must pass from being accessible only through repetition, towards remembering and elaboration. Towards the end of "Confusion of tongues between adults and the child" (1932), Ferenczi states: "If the shocks increase in number during the development of the child, the number and the various kinds of splits in the personality increase too, and soon it becomes extremely difficult to maintain contact without confusion with all the fragments, each of which behaves as a separate personality yet does not know of even the existence of the others. Eventually, it may arrive at a state which – continuing the picture of fragmentation – one would be justified in calling atomisation. One must possess a good deal of optimism not to lose courage when facing such a state, though I hope even here to be able to find threads that can link up the various parts" (p. 165). Atomisation [Atomisierung] and fragmentation [Fragmentierung] are terms employed by Ferenczi in his intent to describe the psychic effects of the traumatic experience and the defences against it.

The adult takes the child by surprise, who remains defenceless as the adult satisfies his sexual and/or aggressive drives. Any prior state of security is eroded. The child used to trust the adult who now takes advantage of him. In order to preserve the adult's good image, the child opts for the splitting of his psyche. He identifies with the aggressor, which eliminates the external aggressor and preserves the tender situation that prevailed before the trauma.

Nonetheless, there is still one requisite for the constitution of the psychic trauma. Analogous to Freud's traumatic theory, in Ferenczi's conceptualisation there are also two moments necessary for the production of trauma, even though they are different from Freud's. In Ferenczi, besides de adult's aggression, another adult's response to this trauma is absolutely relevant. After the traumatic event, a child may go to another significant adult (the mother, for example) to tell her what he has suffered. If there is a denial by this adult, the traumatic effect of the event is, because of this, redoubled. "The mother's disapproval as a dysfunction of language is a traumatic agent that redoubles the early beginnings, which are dysfunctions of the child's libido" (Sabourin, 1984, p. 19, translated). This denial on behalf of the adult crystalizes the trauma in the child.

The traumatic effect of the confusion of tongues can be illustrated schematically as follows:

i There is a state of affairs in which a trusted adult turns into an aggressor and destroys the child's security.

ii The child becomes paralysed by intense fear.

iii The child identifies with the aggressor (at the same time introjecting the aggressor, who disappears as an external entity and becomes intrapsychic). The child wishes to gratify his attacker.

iv In this way, the child succeeds in maintaining the former situation and preserves the good image of the adult.

v The child introjects the adult's sense of guilt.

vi Owing to his guilt, the child feels that his act deserves punishment.

vii The child is already divided, owing to his opposing feelings: he feels at one and the same time innocent and guilty. He is cut off from his own affective states and is pervaded by confusion. One part has recorded the experience, while another seeks to maintain the idea that nothing has happened.

viii The adult's response is a contributory factor to the generation of trauma (Gutiérrez-Peláez, 2009).

The traumatic experience has an effect on memory and remembering. Trauma can produce a block on thoughts and perceptions, a paralyzing of psychic processes. Ferenczi speculates that there is not even an unconscious registering of the experience which is close to Freud's notion of *Verwerfung*, as reread by Lacan's notion of "foreclosure".

The outcome of this 'split in the personality' is that the child denies that anything has happened, in the same way as the adult has denied the event. Due to the fact that nothing has been psychically recorded, there is no possibility of remembering. It is not a matter of repression. It is a trauma, "suffered in early childhood, which has never been experienced consciously and therefore cannot be remembered" (Ferenczi, 1932b, p. 235). Ferenczi also mentions it as a 'fleeting psychosis', a break with reality: "The subject becomes malleable and reacts with fragmentation or even atomization of the personality" (Ferenczi, 1932b, p. 236).

It is by the identification with the aggressor that the child is able to survive. It also preserves the good image of the adult. The psychic split leads the child to be, at the same time, innocent and guilty. "The unpleasure to which this psychic shock gives rise proves impossible to overcome; in other words, the child is unable to deploy a defence that will act on the world about him (i.e., alloplastically) and thereby eliminate the cause of the suffering, nor can he produce a representation matching the suffering whereby some kind of working through or processing might be possible. The trauma immediately results in an overflowing of anxiety in the form of a sense of helplessness that stands in the way of any positive reaction to the situation, such as fight or flight in relation to the external danger" (Gutiérrez-Peláez, 2008). Ferenczi uses the term "intropression", which has been referred to as a precursor of "projective identification" (Cabré, 2011). In "Notes and Fragments" (1934) he writes: "*Child analysis*. Education is super-ego *intropression* (by adults)".

Due to the fact that there is no memory of the event, the psychoanalytic treatment must lead to the repetition of the trauma in a benign and safe environment, in order for him to live it for the first time, inscribe it psychically and find a way to elaborate it (this a clear antecedent of Winnicott's comprehension of the treatment of early trauma) (Gutiérrez-Peláez & Herrera-Pardo, 2017).

Ferenczi refers to the "terrorism of suffering" and uses the German term *Erschütterung* (Ferenczi, 1932b, 1932c). It is a term used by Freud in "Beyond the Pleasure Principle" (1920) to refer to the somatic effects of trauma (its incidence in the body), using the term *Schrek* (freight) instead for the psychic aspect of trauma. In Ferenczi, the word *Erschütterung* is usually translated by "shock" or "psychic shock" and Ferenczi himself mentions it refers to the fact of becoming unfest or unsolid, losing one's form and adopting the form of another without resistance "like a sack of flour" (Ferenczi, 1932b, p. 254). Besides the "terrorism of suffering", incestuous seductions and passionate punishments also have a traumatic potentiality for the child.

Finally, it is worth mentioning that Ferenczi installs a particular viewpoint on his comprehension of the notion of female passivity and female masochism. He believes there is a female function of the analyst in his or her capacity to tolerate unpleasure (Dall'Albero et al., 2020). Due to the fact that a well analysed analyst does not evade the patient's or his own unpleasure, it is possible for him to go further in the patient's experiencing of his original trauma, arriving at deeper healing of the unthinkable experiences that lie deep beneath the surface and are accessible not through words, but through repetitions in the analytic setting. The damaged part of the patient's psyche can be "brought to life" once again through the analytic treatment. Ferenczi tries to go beyond the body-mind dualism by appealing to the notion of "substance", in a sense that could be understood as similar to that of Baruch Spinoza.

# Chapter 12

# Splitting as a psychic defence

In his latest writings, Ferenczi refers to traumas or shocks occurring in the first years of life and speculates that the earliness of the events intensifies the impact it produces in the child's psyche: "The stronger and more destructive the suffering – perhaps also the earlier in life it had to be endured, thus determining an orientation – the larger the circle of interests that must be drawn around the centre of the suffering in order to make it seem meaningful, or even naturally inevitable" (Ferenczi, 1932, p. 31).

A few lines afterwards, in the same entry of the *Diary*, Ferenczi (1932) writes: "A helpless child is mistreated, for example, through hunger. What happens when the suffering increases and exceeds the small person's powers of comprehension? Colloquial usage describes what follows by the expression 'the child comes to be beside itself'. The symptoms of being beside oneself (seen from the outside) are absence of reaction with regard to sensitivity, generalised muscle cramps, often followed by generalised paralysis ('being gone'). If I am to believe what my patients report about similar states, this 'being gone' is not necessarily a state of 'not-being', but rather one of 'not-being-here'" (p. 32). There is a sort of self-abandonment, in which the child feels that what is being inflicted upon him is happening to someone else.

In other parts of his writings, Ferenczi refers to the "autotomy" of consciousness which functions more as an absence of defence than as a proper defence mechanism. Autotomy (not "autonomy"), is a defence present in certain animals in which a part of their body

DOI: 10.4324/9780367854355-12

is split of or abandoned in order to escape from their predators (it is the case of lizards releasing their tails if they are captured by it). Ferenczi describes it in *Thalassa* (1924) as follows: "In certain animals, so the zoologists tell us, there occurs the peculiar reaction known as *autotomy*, consisting in the fact that organs which irritate or otherwise annoy the animal are simply detached from the rest of the body by the action of certain muscles, or, in the literal sense of the word, dropped. There are, for example, worms which are able under such circumstances to extrude the entire intestine from the body; others break into small pieces" (p. 28). Analogously, a child may apply "autotomy" to parts of his or her psyche that have been "caught" by the evil and/or abusive act of an adult. So, in some way, this part of their psyche does not belong to them anymore, it exists as something that is no longer part of their psychic experience. Nonetheless, that absent, traumatised, split off and abandoned part of the self somehow appears in transference, in regressive states of the treatment, but it is necessary to relive the dependence and conditions prior to trauma in the psychoanalytic treatment, but proceeding with absolute caution on the part of the analyst so that his interventions or acts do not lead to the repetition of the same trauma, and to the need to apply the splitting mechanism once again. Instead, the treatment grants the possibility of experiencing the event for the first time and incorporating it into the child's self and psychological experience.

Trauma occurs by an untimely imposition of the adult's libidinal passion or aggression, which are felt by the child as aggression. As Ferenczi referred to in his paper "Introjection and transference" (1909), both of what he calls maternal and paternal hypnosis have an effect on the production of trauma (paternal hypnosis being the absolute submission of the child to the parent's acts, being felt as a death to the child, and maternal hypnosis referring to the abandonment of the mother and the absence of an *other* who could contain and hold the fragmented parts of the psyche), but the most severe effect is when both are present in the events suffered by the child. These are catastrophic for the child and leave him in what Ferenczi speculates to be a permanent state of hypnosis. It is necessary to bear in mind that these acts are perpetrated by a person from which the child expects (and needs) a completely contrary act. This unexpected situation leads to a state of confusion and has not only effects in his or her mind, but in the child's body as well, altering his perception and his sense of self. The insistence of the splitting as a defence can eventually lead to the "atomization" of his personality. It is a mechanism that allows the person to continue alive, thus having abandoned and fragmented his self and having lived as if nothing had happened to him, this with the expense of not integrating the split parts to his experience of self. As they are experiences that have no psychic inscription, not even in the unconscious, they cannot be remembered, but only repeated. As stated in his *Clinical Diary* (1932): "Whenever an emotional reaction is suppressed, interrupted, or repressed, something is actually destroyed in us. The annihilated part of the person falls into a state of decay and decomposes[1]. Should the entire person be prevented from acting, then generalised decomposition ensues, that is to say, death. [...] Total disintegration (death) is just as impossible for it as coming back to life through the influx of vital energies" (Ferenczi, 1932, p. 88). It is the paradox of living in a state of death that has itself allowed the subject to survive. But it is a sort of permanent asymptotic movement towards death, being the accomplishment of death in a future extended *ad infinitum*. Analysis must lead from the agony of death to the recognition of a desire to live (a remnant of the life drives) in the act of maintaining a part of the *self* safe and alive. The subject has adapted through fragmentation, as the lizard has adapted through autotomy, only surviving by the abandonment of a part of his self.

At first, there are no words, no symbolic elaboration, around the lived traumatic experience. It only appears in the treatment in the form of repetition, felt through the transference-countertransference relationship. As the traumatic material is reached, the subject can begin having an experience of that which up until then was only something lived (and not experienced), uniting the fragmented parts of his personality. "What is trauma? 'Concussion', reaction to an 'unbearable' external or internal stimulus in an autoplastic manner (modifying the self) instead of an alloplastic manner (modifying the stimulus). A *neoformation* of the self is impossible without the previous destruction, either partial or total, or dissolution of the former self. A new ego cannot be formed directly from the previous ego, but from fragments, more or less elementary products of its disintegration (Splitting, atomization). The relative strength of the 'unbearable' excitation determines the degree and depth of the ego's disintegration" (Ferenczi, 1932, p. 181). An in-depth reading of Ferenczi's *Diary* and latest writings reveals a traumatic theory that diverges from Freud's conceptualisations and constitutes an original contribution to psychoanalysis.

## Fragmentation

One of Ferenczi's patients, S.I., demands that "I must remove, piece by piece, the fragments of her invading personality; simultaneously she must try to reinsert into her personality the exploded portions of her own person. Following prolonged relaxation and passivity on my part, she now demands: 'you must poke the jellyfish', that is to say, for her sake, I must be somewhat stricter and tougher with her" (p. 48). The metaphor of the jellyfish evokes both the motor reaction of the animal being poked, as well as its vulnerability and lack of consistency, equated here with the state of the psychic functioning of the patient after the severe traumas endured in her lifetime, as well as her defences with which she has managed to survive through a state of fragmentation. Now, as the analysis leads to the reunification of the split parts of her personality, the threat of death and final destruction are brought about with amplified intensity.

Eventually, the traumatic parts embedded in the patient's psyche will cease to exist, their "traumatic fixation" will dissolve, such as Freud suggested with his "excellent comparison with the disintegration of the excavated objects" (p. 50). Once the traumatic elements are brought to the surface from the depths of the unconscious, where they remained silent and unthinkable, but with devastating effects, their consistency dissolves, no longer being the patient's psyche, but the traumatic nucleus itself, that dissolves.

## The Clinical Diary: 'poetry and truth'

As mentioned before, the *Clinical Diary* is one of the most unique documents in the history of psychoanalysis. It is, at the same time, a binnacle of his analysands' analytic processes and sessions, a crucible for the development of bold and ground-breaking ideas on the theory of trauma and technique of psychoanalysis, and a re-count of his analysis and relationship with Freud. Ferenczi wrote to Freud, on May 1, 1932, that he is "immersing myself in a kind of scientific 'Poetry and Truth' from which at some time or other, sometimes I think: definitely, something not worthless will come" (Falzeder & Brabant, 2000, p. 432). Ferenczi reproaches Freud that he gradually lost interest in the therapeutic aspects of psychoanalysis, focusing instead on its theoretical contributions and its insights regarding the functioning of the human mind.

Regarding Ferenczi's constant claims to Freud and his wild transformations of the psychoanalytic technique, specially the "mutual analysis", one could ask: isn't it possible to read in this the excessive demand of an analysand, so desperate and eager of analysis, that he makes of his patient his own analyst? It is true that Ferenczi believed that a cured patient could constitute the true analysts: "'the best analyst is a patient who has been cured'. All other candidate analysts ought to be 'first made ill, then cured and made aware'" (Dupont, p. xxii). There was such a craving in Ferenczi for taking his analysis to the end that he led his analysands to analyse him. This could be a different line of thought to reflect upon Ferenczi's clinical innovations, though it is true that he many times argues and explains that what leads him to the use and development of mutual analysis was the specific psychological needs of the patients with which he practiced it. He did not intend it to be a technique to be applied indistinctly to all analysands, but only to those who had such unique psychological and emotional requirements due to the severity of the traumatic experiences they had had to endure. As he states on June 2, 1932: "mutual analysis: only a last resort! Proper analysis by a stranger, without any obligation, would be better" (p. 115).

There is a progression in Ferenczi's clinical innovations. He had written before about the active technique and its importance in certain cases. Later, he opposes relaxation and neocatharsis to that active technique. He nonetheless finds that there are also contraindications to the use of relaxation. Finally, in the *Clinical Diary*, he presents the innovation that he will name as "mutual analysis". Initially, Ferenczi refers to mutual relaxation, which implies both patient and analyst to fall each in a deep state of relaxation, putting their psychic defences to rest, and the analyst abandoning his role of the "watchman" of the analytic session. "[A]t first sounds totally absurd. What is the use of two people falling into a trance simultaneously and then senselessly talking at cross-purposes, that is, free-associating and also giving vent to their feelings into gestures and expressive movements. Here, as the sole thread offered by previous analytical experience, is the idea (launched if I remember correctly by me): the dialogue of un-consciouses" (p. 84). This idea of the "dialogue of unconsciouses" (or of "dialogue of the unconscious" as Ferenczi proposes in "Psychogenic Anomalies of Voice Production" (1915)), will be frequently revised by different analysts in the history of psycho-analysis, many times without explicitly referencing Ferenczi's authorship. Ferenczi (1932) wrote that "[w]hen two people meet for the first time, an exchange takes place, not only of conscious but of unconscious stirrings. Only analysis could determine for both why inexplicitly to either of them, sympathy or antipathy has developed in either of them. Ultimately, I meant by this that when two people converse, not only a conscious dialogue takes place, but an unconscious one, from both sides. In other words, next to the attention cathected conversation, or parallel to it, a relaxed dialogue is also pursued" (p. 84). Mutual analysis implies that, as its name suggests, in certain moments, the patient takes the place of the analyst and it is the analyst that lies on the couch, analysing with the patient that which has to do with the analysis the analyst is conducting.

In his *Clinical Diary*, Ferenczi insists on the importance of an analyst abandoning his rigid adherence to technique and theory. If the analyst, instead, entrenches in a rigid psychoanalytic model, and cannot tune with the analysand's emotional needs, a great schism opens between them that leaves the patient alone with his psychological precariousness. Once the analyst can abandon his distance and move away from his protected site, he can construct a real relation with the analysand. "If the receptive organ is the analyst's sensibility, the spontaneity and sincerity of his behaviour create the most favourable climate for the analytical situation"

(Cabré, 2020, p. 79). Ferenczi believes that the same technical interventions cannot be used in all cases, but that they must be maintained rigidly in some cases and made flexible in others. The clinical setting is not a procrustean bed to which patients must submit to (Gutiérrez-Peláez & Herrera-Pardo, 2017).

Regarding the psychological functioning of the traumatised child, Ferenczi believes that hate is the prevalent feeling that results from the encounter with the abusive adult that does not take into account the child's psychological functioning and emotional needs. As a result of that traumatic experience, the child can identify with the aggressor, introjecting his feelings of guilt and making them his own.

## The patients in the Clinical Diary

Ferenczi mentions a series of patients throughout his *Diary*, and refers to each with certain initials: "N.G." (who was Greek and is one of the few male patients), "Dm." (whose real name is Clara Thompson, being one of Ferenczi's most important disciples and one the patients he most refers to in his *Diary*), "R.N." (born Leota Loretta Brown, and who changed her name to Elisabeth Severn), "Dr. Dx", "B.", "S.I." (Countess Harriet Sigray), "O.S." (Natalie Rogers), "N.B.", "Case A.", "Case B." (Alicia Lowell), "Patient Ett." (Izette de Forest, who together with Elisabeth Severn and Clara Thompson, constitute the most elaborated clinical cases in his book), "Mrs. E", "Patient U." (also a male), "Dr. S.", "N.H.D." (Roberta (Robbie) Nederhoed), "G." (Anjelika Bijur Frink), "F." and "Patient U." (Theodore (Teddy) Miller). It was mainly with "R.N." that he carried out his mutuality technique, though he practiced it too with other few patients mentioned in his *Diary*. It is thanks to Brennan's (2015) outstanding detective investigation of the *Diary* that we have come much closer to confirming the identities of Ferenczi's patients.

Cabré (2020) mistakenly points out that Ferenczi practiced mutual analysis with Izette de Forest. He had treated de Forest a few years before the beginning of this technical innovation. Cabré's confusion is probably caused by the fact that he refers to patient "B." as being de Forest (p. 354–55), when in fact she is Alice Lowell, who was a friend and lover of de Forest.

Regarding the patients mentioned in the *Diary,* Brennan (2009, 2015) mentions that: "none of the patients in the diary were Hungarian, although one was married to a Hungarian. Most were from an extremely wealthy socioeconomic background, and they were all either born in America or lived in America. The interconnectedness of these patients' relationships with each other is also important. There are important ways in which their lives overlapped and were entangled with each other. It is no surprise the phrase 'six degrees of separation', originated from the famous Hungarian writer and friend of Ferenczi, Frigyes Karinthy (1929), and understanding the interconnectedness of the patients within the Diary further complicates the clinical picture" (Berman, 2015, cited by Brennan, 2015, p. 7). We have mentioned Karinthy before (in Chapter 7) when we displayed Ferenczi's understanding of psychoanalysis as an awakening technique.

Ferenczi speaks of the concept of "Orpha" (Gutiérrez-Peláez, 2008) and understands it as that which keeps us from dying, a protective aspect of the psyche that in certain moments can acquire the form of insanity in itself: madness in the function of allowing the patient to continue living. "Orpha" is a kind of guardian angel that preserves life at all cost, there where the mind has been abandoned (autotomized) as a defence against the unbearable trauma. This idea develops in his analysis of Elisabeth Severn. Ferenczi explicitly mentions Severn in his articles "The principles of relaxation and neocatharsis" (1929): "For this notion [of *psychotic splitting off*] I am partly indebted to discoveries made by our colleague, Elisabeth Severn, which she personally communicated to me" (p. 122), and later again in 1931 ("Child-Analysis in the Analysis of Adults"). Of her, Ernst Jones said she was Ferenczi's "evil genius", probably in the sense applied to the expression by Descartes, as a being that can confuse our senses and makes us perceive a false reality.

In many moments of the *Diary*, Ferenczi is quite critical of Freud and questions his lack of analysis. Ferenczi had offered to analyse Freud, proposal Freud did not concur to. In his *Diary*, Ferenczi writes that "Fr[eud] plays the role of the castrating god, he wants to ignore the traumatic moment of his own castration in childhood; [believing that] he is the only one who does not have to be analysed" (p. 188). These are the tragic coordinates of the psychoanalytic history and training: Freud, as the "discoverer" of the unconscious and founding father of psychoanalysis, had no one before him who could function as his analyst (besides some of his interlocutors (for example, Wilhelm Fliess) that could have allowed him to delve deeper into his auto-analysis) and Ferenczi could not count with a "sufficiently well" analysed analyst with whom he could lead his analysis to its termination.

Throughout his *Diary*, Ferenczi presents rich clinical material that he analyses both regarding the specific circumstances of his patients, as well as what that material reveals about the analytical transference, the patient's psychological and emotional needs, and what these require of the analyst. For example, on January 19, 1932, he refers to one of R.N.'s dreams: "Former patient Dr. Gx. Forces her withered breast into R.N.'s mouth. 'It isn't what I need; too big, empty – no milk'" (p. 13). This dream brings to light both R.N.'s traumatic experiences, her relation with her own patients, and also the analytical relationship with Ferenczi. Can he be for her a nurturing breast or is he a rigid analyst that does not recognise the patient's singular needs no more than a hollow breast forcing its way into the patient's oral void? Regarding the analysis of dreams, it is worth mentioning that Ferenczi introduced novel ideas to the theory of dreams, among them the "traumatolitic" function of certain dreams (Cabré, 2012) which he analysed in the case of his most traumatised patients.

Through mutual analysis with R.N., he believed that the patient was able to integrate aspects of her own traumatic experience in that which Ferenczi, in the place of the patient, could express and link in his own thoughts and affects. Ferenczi alleged patients were quite sensible to the analyst's countertransference. Therefore, by expressing these feelings openly to the patient, the analyst's weaknesses and mistakes, he can allow the analysis to evolve to a much more real basis through which the original trauma could be finally reached.

Mutual analysis is a profound subversion of what Freud insisted on regarding the neutrality of the analyst. The analyst's consent to occupy the role of analysand of his own patient implies a great deal of serious clinical, technical and ethical reflections. For example, is the analyst in the role of patient to submit to the fundamental rule of psychoanalysis? And, if so, would not this lead, in certain moments, to make reference to his associations regarding the analysis of other patients? What happens then with psychoanalytic discretion and confidentiality? In addition, if he renounces to talk about the cases of his patients, would not he be breaking the rule by which it is possible to carry out his own analysis? Wouldn't embracing confidentiality make the analyst, in mutual analysis, unanalysable? This is one of the first limits of mutual analysis: it cannot lead to a full analysis of the analyst and can only be practiced with patients that have the need and the capacity to embrace it.

Another issue that arises is the financial retribution: what if the patient demands payment for her analysis of the analyst? Regarding this, Ferenczi says that "Providing financial help would, however, involve the analysis too much with reality and make separation more difficult" (p. 46).

Ferenczi is critical of the blind spots of his own analysis and can recognise when some of the criticisms that his patients direct to him effectively reach an unresolved issue. So he knows that what the patient grasps of his psychological functioning is true and that it compromises the limits of his function as an analyst. Mutual analysis appears, then, as a way to face and emend this impasse. For example, in the case of R.N., Ferenczi mentions the emotional implications that mutual analysis has for him: "To be more honest, I confess that I would have much preferred to conduct such mutual analysis with my patient S.I., who in spite of more horrifying traumas in her childhood is capable of kindness and selflessness, while in R.N.'s case one always has the feeling that she is constantly pursuing a goal that is finally selfish. To use R.N.'s mode of expression: in R.N. I find my mother again, namely the real one, who was hard and energetic and of whom I am afraid R.N. knows this, and treats me with particular gentleness; the analysis even enables her to transform her own hardness into friendly softness" (p. 45). It was R.N. who most insisted in Ferenczi's concurrence to mutual analysis. It is evident what is demanded of the analyst placed in this position. Nonetheless, in this case, Ferenczi believes that the experience has been beneficial for the transformation of R.N. and has allowed her to build a new form of relation and care for the other through a true analytical relationship. Severn authored books on psychotherapy and continued a long career as a therapist after Ferenczi's death.

Another aspect of Ferenczi's clinical interventions is the time of the sessions. In the case of R.N, for example, some of them could last up to three hours. Ferenczi had referred before to the topic of the time of the analytic session. As it was mentioned before in this book, one of the main reasons that led to the banning of Jacques Lacan from the International Psychoanalytic Association was his use of sessions of variable time. It is this matter of time, and the need to use it for the benefit of the patient and not for the comfort of the analyst, and to orient it towards the awakening of the analysand and not to his sleep, that will constitute an important point of affinity between Ferenczi and Lacan, definitely, both of them *enfants terribles* of psychoanalysis.

Despite this, the difficulties persist for the conceptualisation and possibility of putting mutual analysis into practice. "In the meantime", says Ferenczi, "one must be content with obtaining pieces of analytic insight from the patients in scattered fragments, and not allow them to concern themselves with our person any more than is necessary for their analysis" (p. 45). This might be, at this point, the most elemental distinction and emphasis of the polemic technique of mutual analysis: it should not consist in a device for the analyst to analyse himself (he has his own analyst for that), but only to analyse those aspects of his psyche that have to do with the patient's analysis. But even with this precision, which we could call the "fundamental rule" of mutual analysis, we can see how slippery the path can be and one preserves the impression that Ferenczi is nonetheless interested in the analysis of his own unconscious through his patients.

In his *Diary*, Ferenczi also mentions traumatic experiences he was subjected to in his infancy. While carrying out his mutual analysis with R.N., Ferenczi mentions that "While telling the 'analyst' about this, I submerged myself deeply in the reproduction of infantile experiences; the most evocative image was the vague appearance of female figures, probably servant girls from earliest childhood, then the image of a corpse, whose abdomen I was opening up, presumably in the dissecting room; linked to this the mad fantasy that I was being pressed into this wound in the corpse. Interpretation: the after-effect of passionate scenes, which presumably did take place, in the course of which a housemaid probably allowed me to play with her breasts, but then pressed my head between her legs so that I became frightened and felt I was suffocating. This is the source of my hatred for females: I want to dissect them for it, that is, to kill them. This is why my mother's accusation 'You are my murderer' cut to the heart and led to (1) a compulsive desire to help anyone who is suffering, especially women; and (2) a flight from situations in which I would have to be aggressive. This inwardly the feeling that, in fact, I am a good chap, also exaggerated my reactions of rage, even at trivial affronts, and finally exaggerated reactions of guilt to the slightest lapse" (p. 61). These extensive intimate associations linked to a premature sexual experience, with condensed erotic arousal and the fear of death, are rich elements to reflect upon Ferenczi's psychological functioning. He lets us know that this constituted for him a traumatic experience. There is a deferred action in which his mother's words are traumatic as well and become a nucleus of his relation with others and, even, to what drives him to become an analyst. It is both the solution he finds to face the trauma and the limit to moving further in the analysis of his patients. Becoming aware of this fantasmatic functioning can allow him to understand when he is acting for the best benefit of his patient and when he is acting defensively in order to "not know" about his traumatic nucleus (Gutiérrez-Peláez, 2021).

Some entries later in his *Diary*, Ferenczi goes back once again to the topic of his analysis. "This capacity of mine was unmasked in the course of mutual analysis as my sense of guilt at the death of a sister (diphtheria) two years younger than myself. The reaction against it makes me unsympathetic toward the sick; this I overcome by showing excessive kindness, medical interest, and tact (surely exaggerated)" (p. 121). Through these insights in his analysis, Ferenczi can isolate more clearly what is at stake for him in his most fundamental aspects of his relation to others: his election of medicine, his work as a clinician and as an analyst. In addition, it is through the latter that he is able to look into the void of these traumatic experiences. It is possibly a contribution of Ferenczi, in his reading and redefinition of Freud's concept of counter-transference, that the analyst can use it to dissolve his own resistances and to get hold and deeply understand the emotional and unconscious functioning of the patient.

## Note

1 Fergusson (2015) has developed the hypothesis of psychosis as a process of psychic decomposition and decay.

# Chapter 13

# The repression of Ferenczi's work and the return of the repressed

As mentioned in Chapter 1, Ferenczi was subjected to a forced disappearance, despite having been, as it is possible to see after his resurrection, a key figure and influence in the psycho-analytic movement and of the intellectual establishment of the XXth century. On page 85 of the last volume of the Standard Edition of Freud's works, where the "Bibliography of other specialised authors" is listed, it is possible to see that he refers to Ferenczi's work sixty-nine times in his oeuvre. The Freudian references are distributed among thirty-four of his texts and thirty-four of Ferenczi's papers are mentioned. "These figures place him as the author most alluded to [by Freud]" (Jiménez Avello, 1998, p. 28) and of which Freud addresses the largest number of works. Freud (1976/1923) wrote, on the occasion of Ferenczi's 50th birthday, that his analytical writings "are universally known and appreciated [...]. Books and pamphlets written in the Hungarian language have had new editions and have made the analysis familiar to the cultured circles o Hungary" (p. 288–89).

Freud (1976/1914) paid tribute to this analyst, patient, inter locutor and colleague of his: "Hungary, so close to Austria geo graphically and so distant from it scientifically, until now has no provided psychoanalysis but a single collaborator, S. Ferenczi; bu such that it is valid for an entire association" (p. 32) and, in the obituary of 1933, he refers to Ferenczi's writings that "made al analysts his disciples" (Freud, 1976/1933, p. 227).

DOI: 10.4324/9780367854355-13

Kosztolányi wrote, after Ferenczi's death that (quoted by Mészàros, 2000): "He suffered from a kind of intense restlessness, from a childish humour, from an insatiable curiosity [...] He was very interested in linguistics, theatre, new ideas, gossip, any human matter [...] No one could come up with something so seemingly improbable that he could not find something probable in it and no one could produce a sufficiently supported truth in which he could not insert a halo of doubt [...] He even considered man himself as an enigma that could not be described with one or another psychological paradigm" (p. 54). The biography of Freud written by Ernest Jones (1953) left as a legacy the conception that, during the 1930s, Ferenczi was in a psychotic condition and the work of his final years a product of a troubled mind: "[Ferenczi] gradually towards the end of his life, developed psychotic manifestations that revealed themselves in, among other ways, a turning away from Freud and his doctrines. The seed of a destructive psychosis, invisible for so long, at last, germinated (p. 47; for this topic also see Bonomi, 1999). The handling that was given after his death to his 1932 article "Confusion of languages between the adult and the child", reveals to what extent an active work was done by various psychoanalysts of the time to exclude his work from public knowledge (Masson, 1984; Rachman, 1989; Sylwan, 1984; Hidas, 1993; Gutiérrez-Peláez, 2018).

Regarding the history of Ferenczi's work in other languages, it is noted that "the last English 'edition' of his work was made in the 1950s from translations made for the most part around 1920. Unfortunately, many of them appear today badly dated and inaccurate. The edition is also incomplete since many of the first articles in Hungarian, some German conferences and most of the revisions still remain without translation. Finally, the work is not chronologically ordered, does not have cross-references, nor is it sufficiently edited to explain the forgotten details of some old debates" (Stanton, 1997, p. 57). The *Clinical Diary* (1985/1932c and 1997/1932d), appeared first in French, and only until 1985, translated by Judith Dupont. That same year it appeared in Spanish, translated by Beatriz Castillo in the edition of the editorial Conjectural and then, in 1997, with a translation by

José Luis Etcheverri, in an edition of Argentinean editorial Amorrortu entitled *Sin simpatía no hay curación* [*Without sympathy there is no cure*] (1932d), title taken from a note on one of the entries of the Diary. It was not until 1988 that an edition of the *Clinical Diary* was published for the first time in German, the language in which it was originally written. That year, an English edition was also launched for the first time, the translation of which had been carried out by Michael Balint, but in this edition published by Harvard Press, the fragments that Balint himself had excluded from the original appeared restored (the other editions, thanks to the Dupont's work, include that material as well). In Spanish, for its part, in 1959 the Horné publishing house published *Sex and Psychoanalysis* in Argentina and, in 1967, Paidós published *Theory and Technique of Psychoanalysis* (Sabsay Foks, 2011, p. 429). His complete works to Spanish were translated by Francisco Javier Aguirre and published by the Espasa-Calpe publishing house. The first three volumes of this edition appeared in 1981 and the fourth in 1984. In the latter, however, the *Clinical Diary* is not included. In 2012 (Gutiérrez-Peláez, 2012, p. 263–276), a translation to Spanish of the article "*Sprachverwirrung zwischen den Erwachsenen und dem Kind*" (1933/1932b) ["Confusion of languages between the adult and the child"] was published, correcting errors present in previous translations, due to the fact that they were mostly made from translations of the English and French translations. Currently, Judit Mészáros is leading a project for the publication of Ferenczi's complete works in English and Hungarian. The English edition will include 10 volumes and, in Hungarian, 7 volumes. We hope to have it available in the near future and it will undoubtedly contribute to new readings and studies of Ferenczi's writings.

Szokolszky (2016) mentions that "Actually, the past is making its way into the present, as it is the case with Ferenczi's legacy. Since the publication of his *Clinical Diary* in 1985 and the Freud–Ferenczi correspondence (Brabant, Falzeder and Giampieri-Deutsch, 1993, Falzeder, Brabant and Giampieri-Deutsch, 1996) his work has been gradually re-evaluated and given substantial acknowledgement (Rudnytsky et al., 1996, Szekacs-Weisz and Keve, 2012).

The opening of the *Sándor Ferenczi Center* at the *New School for Social Research* (New York) in 2009, and the Budapest-based international Ferenczi Center and Ferenczi house in 2011 also attest to the reinforced interest in his work. Ferenczi is now considered as having initiated a paradigm shift in psychoanalysis that has made his work highly important for post-Freudian psychoanalysis and contemporary psychotherapy at large (Rudnytsky, 1996; Giampieri-Deutsch, 1996; Curtis, 1996). The work of Melanie Klein, Margaret Mahler, René Spitz, and Harry Harlow is clearly recognised as having roots in Ferenczi's approach to psychoanalysis (Klein was Ferenczi's analysand; Mahler and Spitz, being also Hungarians, were influenced by Hungarian psychoanalysis, see Vikár, 1996)" (p. 46).

It is to be assumed that Ferenczi will continue to give future generations something to talk about and that he will continue to be a source of love and hate. As his work continues to be revised and published, new contemporary readings of classic and novel, preanalytic and late texts will shed new light on the doctrine of psychoanalysis. Mészáros, for example, first published in 1999 an edition of Ferenczi's preanalytical writings (Erös, 2004, p. 128), which have been the subject of few studies. In 2012, during the *International Ferenczi Conference*: "The Faces of Trauma", in Budapest, Hungary, Emanuel Berman (University of Haifa, Israel) and Martha Fülöp (Institute of Cognitive Neuroscience and Psychology of the Hungarian Academy of Sciences) presented a paper on Ferenczi, entitled "The Unknown Poet: Sándor Ferenczi", which was inspired by a series of poems recently found by Blaise Plasztory, grandson of Gizella Ferenczi's brother. Written in a single notebook and some adorned with his drawings, it was never intended for publication and yet preserved. There are a total of 120 poems that Ferenczi wrote between his 26 and 28 years. The sentence of the researchers: "Ferenczi was a very bad poet!", suggests that it will not be his case to be rediscovered as a poet and his literary writings of those years seem to promise little. His drawings and poems would perhaps fit into the "Outsider art" genre. Despite this, they undoubtedly reveal particular aspects of their author - an intense, visceral, jealous lover - and the authors have planned to publish some of these poems in the future, accompanied by a study on Ferenczi's life during this period. Anyway, it would be unfair to disregard Ferenczi's "poetry" through this marginal examples. A poet is, amongst other things, someone who can transform words from its common use and articulate and blend them in a novel way that can lead to understanding and grasping the sense of reality and existence that is elusive to thought and comprehension. His probing into the traumatic dimension of language is what certainly inserts him into his poetic talent and were we can more clearly find the poetic aspect of the psychoanalytic act. His *Diary* was, as he mentioned in his correspondence with Freud, his "scientific 'poetry and truth'". As we will see below, Hungarian writer Sándor Márai praised his poetic thinking: "he knew what poets know: to feel that inexpressible something that constitutes the true secret of a soul".

Ferenczi died of pernicious aneamia on May 22, 1933, at 2:30 p.m., just before his sixtieth birthday. He was buried two days later in the Farkastret Jewish Cemetery in Budapest and his name is accompanied by brief words written in capital letters that read: "A PSZICHOANALIZIS MAGYAR MEGALAPITOJA" ["THE FOUNDER OF PSYCHOANALYSIS IN HUNGARY"].

Given Ferenczi's pivotal role at the epicentre of the Hungarian intelligentsia, several of the greatest thinkers of that time wrote about his untimely death. This is the case of Márai, who published a short obituary entitled "Alive and Dead". Márai's writing on the death of Ferenczi is of astonishing vitality and covers different aspects of Ferenczi. Regarding his personality, Márai wrote "[Ferenczi] ordered one of his family members that if he died by chance, they should not believe it immediately, that they shake him with force [...]. It was what he thought of the body; as if it were a clock that stops from time to time and has to be shaken to keep it going. In this cold arrogance, in which he gave instructions to his family in the event of his own death, man is completely reflected in his whole being". Márai also refers to the subversive and marginal character of psychoanalysis. The lucidity regarding this matter is astonishing and of great historical relevance. Márai says: "Why, then, does everyone hate this new science with the same infinite force: the Bolsheviks consider it 'anti-revolutionary'

Hitler and his people, harmful and revolutionary; American bourgeois criticism sees it as 'Jewish science; the Church put it on the *Index*, because it 'breaks' the unity of the spirit, 'erodes' faith?" It is pointed out to what extent psychoanalysis, from its origins, has been perceived as subversive for political institutions and systems and, indeed, it has been found on different occasions how, when psychoanalysis is too comfortable in one institution, it is probably because it is something else that is being carried out in the name of psychoanalysis (Fergusson, 2015). Freud had already announced it in a letter he addressed to Reik on the occasion of his trip to the United States, where he warned him against those colleagues for whom "psychoanalysis is nothing more than a servant of psychiatry" (1938, cited by Gay, 1988, p. 701).

The fundamental role of Ferenczi in the thought and in the intelligentsia of the time is another important point in Márai's obituary. Regarding this, Márai is forceful: "Ferenczi belongs to the gallery of the figures of the Hungarian intelligentsia of the century, at least as much as his teacher and friend Freud belongs to the history of the twentieth century [...]. The importance of the discovery [of the unconscious] has the same value as that of gunpowder, the printing press or the theory of relativity. This was what Ferenczi made present [...] Without Freud, and without what Ferenczi polished and added, it would be impossible to imagine the intellectual radiography of this century". These short fragments allow a glimpse of the transcendental dimension that Ferenczi played for the Hungarian intelligentsia of his time and the way in which he was perceived by his contemporaries. Quite a contrast with what was, in the years that followed, an absolute forgetfulness of his work, until he returned to the debates of psychoanalysis in the same way as the return of the repressed (Gutiérrez-Peláez, 2018).

Márai's work was also the object of neglect and repression in his country. When Ferenczi died, Márai was a young writer in his thirties who already enjoyed great literary prestige. As his biographer Ernö Zeltner (2001) recounts, at that time "this novelist already had a considerable set of readers who increased mainly thanks to his journalistic activity. It was increasingly common to come across Márai's name in public life: he had reached a position and was leading an active life" (p. 97). Márai, a haughty critic of the totalitarian regimes and an opponent of the German occupation in Hungary, ended his days in exile in the United States (San Diego, California), being his work censored in his country. On February 21, 1989, Márai took his own life, without having been able to see what happened at the end of that year and which undoubtedly would have delighted him: the fall of the Berlin Wall. Six days before shooting himself in the head, he wrote a heart-breaking journal entry, the only handwritten note of his diary: "I'm waiting for the draft; I'm not in a hurry, but I don't want to put off anything because of my doubts. The time has come" (Márai, 1999, p. 209).

The obituary written by Márai was published for the first time in the newspaper *Brassói Lapok* on June 14, 1933. It was released again in 1999 in *Thalassa* Magazine and in 2000 in Judit Mézaros' book *In Memoriam Sándor Ferenczi* and published in Spanish for the first time in 2013 (Gutiérrez-Peláez, 2013).

In her autobiographical notes, Melanie Klein wrote: "There is much that I have to thank Ferenczi for. One thing that he conveyed to me, and strengthened in me, was the conviction in the existence of the unconscious and its importance for mental life. I also enjoyed being in touch with somebody who was a man of unusual gifts. He had a streak of genius" (Grosskurth, 1986, p. 73). These quotes regarding Ferenczi's death give us a glimpse of his undeniable importance in the history of the 20th century. As we will see in the following chapters, the richness of his thought continues inspiring new readings of his work and constitutes a fundamental piece for the future of psychoanalysis.

# Chapter 14

# Ferenczi's legacy and place in the world today

## The Budapest school of psychoanalysis

As stated by Mészáros (2009): "He [Ferenczi] and the members of the Budapest School represented not only Hungarian roots but also the values, the scholarly approach, and the creativity characteristic of Central Eastern Europe in the first half of the 20th century. They were fundamental in supplying the world with a great many scholars and artists – among them, nuclear physicists Edward Teller and Leo Szilard, mathematician John von Neumann, father of the modern computer, and writer Sándor Márai; the latter two were close to Ferenczi" (p. 69). Ferenczi created the first *Hungarian Psychoanalytical Society* in 1913. As we have seen before, it was a diverse and heterogeneous Society which invested the Hungarian intelligentsia with original insights and a fertile space for creation. Ignotus, an important literary figure in Hungary at the time, "described early psychoanalysis as spread by Ferenczi in this way: 'The next day we were already thinking differently than we had been the day before'" (Ignotus, 1933/2000, p. 38, cited by Mészáros, 2009, p. 72). Unfortunately, a series of political events in the turmoil of the first half of the 20th century eventually led Hungary to lose the potential it once had at becoming the centre of the psychoanalytic movement. "The end of World War I brought with it the collapse of the Austro-Hungarian monarchy. Having been on the losing side, Hungary lost two-thirds of its territory in the peace treaty that followed. Other dramatic changes also took place between 1918 and 1920. In fact,

DOI: 10.4324/9780367854355-14

in the space of only a year and a half, the monarchy crumbled and the 'Aster Revolution' – based on the liberal, radical opposition of the First World War' – brought about the creation of a short-lived, first Hungarian Republic, which was unable to steady itself amid both the domestic and international political power struggles surrounding it. It thus gave way to the Soviet Republic that lasted for several months, which was, in turn, followed by a backlash of rightist White Terror. Against changes and disturbances of such proportions, the potential for Budapest playing a central role in the psychoanalytic movement was utterly lost" (Mészáros, 2009, p. 73). The increase in antisemitism, the hunting of political dissidents and the deteriorating economic situation, eventually led the Jewish, liberal, leftist intellectual to immigrate to other countries. Many of them emigrated to Berlin and Vienna. Sándor Rado, member of the Hungarian Psychoanalytical Society, played an important role in creating a Psychoanalytic Institute in Berlin in 1920 and, later, in the 1930s, an institute in New York after his emigration to America. Sadly, the efforts in Berlin would eventually go array after Hitler's rise to power in 1933.

Following Ferenczi's death, the extension of anti-Semitic politics obliged the remaining analyst to flee to countries who were open to receive them. After the annexation of Austria to Nazi Germany (known as the *Anschluss*), the *American Psychoanalytic Association* played an active role in aiding the analyst to leave Hungary to America. Many of these Hungarian analysts had outstanding influence in the development of psychology and psychoanalysis, both in Europe and the United States. Among them we could mention Melanie Klein, Margaret Mahler, Michael Balint, Sándor Rado, Franz Alexander, and David Rapaport.

After WWII, Hungary was under a communist rule for four decades. The psychology in Hungary followed the Soviet model during those periods (Szokolszky, 2016). As stated by Judit Mészáros[1], psychoanalysis was prohibited during the communist regimes. "Psychoanalysis could no longer be practiced openly until the mid-1960s" (Szokolszky, 2016, p. 40). As most of the male psychoanalysts were physicians, they dedicated their practice to other branches of medicine. Female psychoanalysts, on the other hand, continued practicing in secrecy for forty years, which gives psychoanalysis in Hungary its imprint of feminine social and political resistance.

In 1988, a group of Hungarian psychoanalysts founded the *Sándor Ferenczi Society*[2] in Budapest. Through this association, they have contributed to revitalising Hungarian psychoanalysis and to continue the psychoanalytic ideas of Ferenczi. Other institutions and organisations created to preserve the work of Sándor Ferenczi and to continue the advancement of his thought include *The International Sándor Ferenczi Network (ISFN)*[3], with headquarters in Firenze, Italy, and directed by psychoanalyst and Ferenczi scholar Carlo Bonomi. The *ISFN* organises the International Sándor Ferenczi conference that takes place every three years.

In 2011, both the *Sándor Ferenczi Society* and the *ISFN* were able to mobilise an important international cooperation of 271 donors, contributions with which they were able to buy an apartment in Ferenczi's former Naphegy Villa in Budapest[4]. Ferenczi lived in this villa from 1930 to his death in 1933, having been the location of his most bold and original writings.

## Sándor Ferenczi Center in the New School of Social Research

The *Sándor Ferenczi Center* was founded in 2008 in the *New School of Social Research* in New York. It was there that Sándor Ferenczi lectured for four months during his stay in the US during 1926, having been invited by Alvin Saunders Johnson, cofounder of the *New School*. The Center is currently directed by Dr. Adrienne Harris and Dr. Miriam Steele. As stated in their website: "The goals of the New School Ferenczi Center include (1) sponsoring lectures, conferences, and workshops relevant to Ferenczi's legacy of clinical innovation, (2) promoting Ferenczi's legacy of social and political progressivism, and (3) contributing to the ongoing vitality of psychoanalysis as a cultural, intellectual, therapeutic discipline".[5]

The *New School* also became an important representative of "relational psychoanalysis", which became mainstream in North America, with representatives of this school in their directives, such as Lewis Aron, Jeremy Safran and Adrienne Harris. Stephen A. Mitchell is often mentioned as one of the most influential figures of "relational psychoanalysis". As stated by Gail Newman (2020), "Ferenczi's impact has been greatest in the arena of relational and intersubjective psychoanalysis, though some have put his ideas in conversation with Freud, Winnicott, Groddeck, and Lacan. See specially Borgogno, Stanton, Gutiérrez-Peláez" (p. 19).

In Latin America, Ferenczi's legacy has also hit in fertile ground. One of the most prominent actions has been the creation of the *Asociación Latinoamericana Sandor Ferenczi* [*Latin American Association Sándor Ferenczi*][6], thanks to the sustained effort of the renowned Chilean Ferenczian analyst Juan V. Gallardo. Gallardo has been able to create an important international and regional network that continually publishes articles and reviews regarding Ferenczi's (and Groddeck's) work, as well as translations to Spanish of articles and books both of and about Ferenczi. Since a few years ago, Gallardo has embraced the project of building a sanatorium in the south of Chile, called *Thalassa*, and inspired both in Groddeck's sanatorium in Baden-Baden and in Ferenczi's work.

Ferenczi's influence has disseminated massively, with important scholars and analysts worldwide. Academic events and conferences are carried out both in North and South America and in Europe. It is also interesting that his work has been able to inspire the arts. It is the case of filmmaker Emm Cooper who, in 2012 presented the short film entitled "Confusion of Tongues"[7] and which is inspired in the homonymous paper by Ferenczi. It is a lucid and personal interpretation by the artist of Ferenczi's article, which grasps the theoretical comprehension present in the argument, as well as the emotional impact of the adult's passion over the child's tenderness. Nonetheless, the film leaves us with hope on how it is possible to find a way out of infantile traumas.

As beautifully stated by Mészáros (2009): "Maybe many of you share some of my sense of who Ferenczi was. He knew how to watch, how to keep quiet, and how to listen. He could endure the tension created by uncertainties without giving rapid, prejudiced responses. He respected human sovereignty and focused the tools of psychoanalysis on developing an autonomous personality.

He avoided professional hypocrisy, and his tolerance and ability to cooperate made it possible to create real interdisciplinary connections. After half a century of apparent death, the intellectual spirit of Ferenczi has been revived by the unwavering commitment and hard work of two generations of professionals throughout the world" (p. 86). It is the vitality of his spirit and of his legacy that makes this freewheeler and loose piece a fundamental gear for the future of psychoanalysis and why the continuation of the lucid and enriching path opened by him should be embraced.

## Notes

1  Personal conversation.
2  http://ferencziSándor.hu/
3  https://www.Sándorferenczi.org/the-ferenczi-house/
4  https://www.Sándorferenczi.org/the-ferenczi-house/
5  https://blogs.newschool.edu/Sándor-ferenczi-center/
6  https://www.alsf-chile.org/ferenczi-hoy.html
7  http://www.emcooper.com/film/confusion-of-tongues/

# Chapter 15

# What is the relevance of Ferenczi in the future?

Our clinical experience has shown us, once and again that symptoms change with time and that there are particular "societies and their discontents" in every epoch. Being able to effectively respond to the challenges of each time requires both a clear orientation on the principles of psychoanalysis and a flexibility to intervene in the novel clinical aspects we encounter. Crisis such as that of Covid-19, during which we wrote this book, lectured at universities and treated our analysands (in our consultation offices and/or online), show us how we do not know what the conditions of each epoch will be. Online treatments were seen as a heresy by many analystes and to some it still is, but to others, us included, it is a clear example of the openness and creativity needed to allow psychoanalysis to prevail. Those are the sort of situations that force us to identify which are really the fundamental basis of the psychoanalytic technique. Our function is not to preserve the past, in a melancholy of the "good old days", but to be able to intervene with the conditions of possibility, with ethics and in the benefit of the people we treat. How not to lose ourselves in the use of technical innovations? We believe that Ferenczi did no consider that there was a final guarantee for this, but what could be the best protector, both for the analyst and the analysand, was the analysis of the analyst. This desire to take the analysis to its final consequences, to reach its termination and to the exhaustion of the unconscious, continues to be the most important piece in the training of analysts. There is no final guarantee for this, but it is through this process that an analyst can lead his treatments in the benefit of the

DOI: 10.4324/9780367854355-15

unveiling of the unconscious and not in the satisfaction of his sadistic or masochistic unconscious tendencies.

Ferenczi also shows, as did most of the analysts of the first and second generation of psychoanalysts, a political compromise. He believed that it was not that psychoanalysis could be done in any conditions, but that the psychoanalytic discoveries could be taken to different social estates, such as education, breeding, family relations, governance, amongst others. He believed, as Freud, that the best destiny for psychoanalysis was not to become "a servant of psychiatry", as it did effectively become in many countries and societies worldwide (Fergusson, 2015), but a fertile and always fresh science that could be a valid interlocutor with other sciences, arts, academy, common citizens and elaborated intellectuals.

Also, those who should and could benefit from psychoanalysis are not only people with the necessary material and economic settings, but people of all social conditions and so-called "mental illnesses". The project of the psychoanalytic free clinics (Danto, 2005), which was in great part hampered by the political events that led to WWII, is still a relevant project. In the current crisis of mental health worldwide, the costs linked to labour incapacities produced by mental health issues, and the impossibility of mental health institutions and services to respond effectively to the demands of the population, show the need for both accessible services and well-trained professionals, not just trained in branded psychotherapies, or in techniques that are thought to be effective for clustered populations, but that can adequately respond to the specific needs of the consultants.

Finally, all of the above allowed Ferenczi to be really inclusive and to not discriminate against people that have been diagnosed with conditions that were wrongly supposed not to be susceptible to psychoanalysis. He accepted the challenge to force himself to produce modifications in how we intervene and bring about unthought-of dynamics that require a sympathetic analyst that will not retrieve from these highly demanding requirements but, will find the way to lodge that singular rarity of the analysand. That is the essence of his legacy to us.

# Epilogue

The process of writing this book came for us both as a desire and as the fulfilment of a debt with a most prominent figure of the psychoanalytic history, which had meant for us inspiration on our independent careers. Professor Alberto Fergusson, psychiatrist and psychoanalyst member of the *International Psychoanalytic Association* (IPA), developed in the 1980s a model called "Accompanied Self-rehabilitation" (ASR), which was inspired in Freudo-Marxist ideals of the Frankfurt School, the spirit of the antipsychiatry movement of the seventies, and the original proposal of the Freudian free clinics (Danto, 2005). In his books *Imaginary Letters to Freud and other essays* (2015a) and *Accompanied Self-rehabilitation* (2015b) (with prologue by Courtnay Harding), Fergusson described his more than 30 years of work in the development of his ASR model, which was initially applied as a psychosocial intervention for homeless people diagnosed with schizophrenia, and later for the treatment of a wider population with various conditions. As was the experience of Sándor Ferenczi, Fergusson evidenced through his clinical work with people diagnosed with schizophrenia, the need to implement modifications in the psychoanalytic technique and that it is the technique that must adapt to the patient's needs and not the patient to the clinicians way of functioning.

The model has been an inspiration for the development of other ones fit for the particular conditions of the Colombian armed conflict, being applied to negotiation in peace processes (due to Fergusson's designation during President (and Nobel Peace Prize winner) Juan Manuel Santos' presidency as government delegate in the peace talks with the *National Liberation Army* – ELN – guerrilla group in Quito, Ecuador) and to the construction of truth and understanding (as an adviser of Colombia's Truth Commission, 2019–2022). In these diverse scenarios, the four basic principles of ASR are preserved: (1) ignorance as a recognition of what we do not know; (2) taking leadership of one's own process; (3) becoming an expert in oneself; and (4) redesigning one's life system (Fergusson, 2015b).

Miguel Gutiérrez-Peláez, psychologist and psychoanalyst member of the *World of PSychoanalysis Association* (WAP-AMP), first came in contact with Ferenczi's work due to his questions regarding the functioning of the mind of so-called "psychotic patients", question opened both by his work in his private practice and in psychiatric institutions. This led him to develop his master's and doctoral thesis on Sándor Ferenczi's work and has published numerous articles on Ferenczi in indexed journals, including the book *Confusion of Tongues. A Return to Sándor Ferenczi,* published in 2018 by Routledge.

On August 27, 2015, we created the *Center for Psychosocial Studies* (CEPSS) within the Universidad del Rosario, in Bogotá, Colombia, which has since then been directed by professor Fergusson. The centre, in which teachers, researchers and students from the Universidad del Rosario have participated, has maintained a great interest in the productions of the first and second generation of psychoanalysts (Sigmund Freud, Sándor Ferenczi, Wilhelm Reich, Jacques Lacan, among others), as well as other thinkers and intellectuals who made their approach or their contributions to psychoanalysis and 20th-century thought (such as Lou Andreas Salomé, Jeremy Bentham, Karl Marx, Martin Heidegger, Mikhail Bakhtin, Charles Sanders Peirce and Hans-Georg Gadamer).

Ferenczi's work on the training of the analyst, the comprehension of trauma, the development of the clinical setting, the treatment of psychosis, the work with marginalised and stigmatised groups, among others, continue being an inspiration and orientation of our centre, both for the work in classical clinical settings and outside the couch, from psychosocial interventions with marginalized and stigmatised groups, to the mediation and dialogues leading to the construction of peace. Going through Ferenczi's work, once again, we get the feeling that it is inexhaustible and that new moments of clarity are experienced through his creative thought and ground-breaking ideas. We hope the readers that have followed us until the end will find themselves curious about going to his writings and lectures (for the first time or once again) and allow themselves to be amazed and moved by the novelties that await in those lines, like those precious stones evoked in the metaphor of the mine of the unconscious.

# References

Balint, M. (1968). *Prefase. Sándor Ferenczi. Complete Works.* [Francisco Javier Aguirre, translator]. Madrid: Espasa Calpe. 1981.

Barzilai, S. (1997). History is not the past: Lacan's critique of Ferenczi, *Psychoanalytical Review, 84*(4), 553–572.

Bonomi, C. (1999). Flight into sanity: Jones's allegation of Ferenczi's mental deterioration reconsidered. *International Journal of Psycho-Analysis 80*: 507–542.

Bokanowski, T., *Sándor Ferenczi. Psychanalystes d' aujourd' hui.* Paris: Presses Universitaires de France. 1997.

Brennan, B.W. (2009). Ferenczi's forgotten messenger: The life and work of Izette de Forest. *American Imago, 66*(4), 427–455. doi:10.1353/aim.0.0071.

Brennan, B.W. (2015). Decoding Ferenczi's *Clinical Diary*: Biographical notes. *The American Journal of Psychoanalysis, 75*, 5–18.

Cabré, M.L. (comp.) (2011). From introjection to intropression: Evolution of a theoretical concept and its consequences for psychoanalytic technique. *American Journal of Psychoanalysis, 71*, 321–328. https://doi-org.ez.urosario.edu.co/10.1057/ajp.2011.38

Cabré, M.L. (2020). *Autenticidad y reciprocidad. Un diálogo con Ferenczi [Authenticity and Reciprocity. A Dialogue with Sándor Ferenczi].* Madrid: Spain: Biebel.

Cabré, M. (2021). Paper presented at the International Conference "Ferenczi: Faces of Trauma". Budapest, Hungary. May-June.

Castillo Mendoza, C.A. (2005). Perspectivas sociales del psicoanálisis. La relación entre lo psíquico y lo social en Sandor Ferenczi. [Social perspectives of psychoanalysis. The relationship between the psychic and the social in Sandor Ferenczi.]. *Clínica y análisis grupal, 94*(27–1), 65–69.

Danto, E.A. (2005). *Freud's Free Clinics. Psychoanalysis and Social Justice, 1918-1938*. New York, USA: Columbia University Press.

Dall'Albero, P., Ferretti, P. & Mirabile, F. (2020). Transmisiones de afectos y vivencias en la relación [Transmission of affects and experiences in the relation] (pp. 247–347). In: *Autenticidad y reciprocidad. Un diálogo con Ferenczi [Authenticity and Reciprocity. A Dialogue with Sándor Ferenczi]*. (Cabré, L.M. comp.). Madrid: Spain: Biebel.

Dupont, J., editor (1985). *The Clinical Diary of Sándor Ferenczi*. [Balint M., Zarday Jackson N., translators]. Cambridge, MA: Harvard UP, 1988.

Dupont, J. (1998). The concept of trauma according to Ferenczi and its effects on subsequent psychoanalytical research. *International Forum of Psychoanalysis*, 7, 235–240.

Erös, F. (2018). Ferenczi, Freud, anarcho-communism, and mass psychology. Draft of the paper to be presented at the 13th International Sándor Ferenczi Conference: Ferenczi in Our Time – and – A Renaissance of Psychoanalysis, May 3–6, 2018, Florence, Italy.

Erös, F. (2004). The Ferenczi cult: its historical and political roots. *International Forum of Psychoanalysis*, *13*(1–2), 121–128, 10.1080/08037060410024032.

Evans, D. (1996). *An introduction dictionary of Lacanian psychoanalysis*. London: Routledge.

Falzeder, E. & Brabant, E., (Eds.) (2000). *The correspondence of Sigmund Freud and Sándor Ferenczi, vol. 3*, 1920–1933. Cambridge, MA: Belknap.

Fergusson, A. (2015a). *Cartas imaginarias a Freud y otros ensayos [Imaginary Letters to Freud and other essays]*. Colombia: Universidad del Rosario.

Fergusson, A. (2015b). *Accompanied Self-Rehabilitation*. Colombia: Universidad del Rosario.

Ferenczi, S. (1902). Homosexualitas feminina. *Gyógyászat 11*, 167–168.

Ferenczi, S. (1909). Introjection and transference. In: *First contributions to psycho-analysis*, Jones E., translator (pp. 35–93.) London: The Hogarth Press and the Institute of Psycho-Analysis, 1952.

Ferenczi, S. (1913). A little chanticleer, In: *First Contributions to Psychoanalysis* (pp. 240–252). London: The Hogarth Press and the Institute of Psycho-Analysis, 1952.

Ferenczi, S. (1915). Psychogenic anomalies of voice production. In: *Further Contributions* (pp. 105–109). London: Karnac, 2002.

Ferenczi, S. (1924). *Thalassa. A Theory of Genitality*. London: Karnac, 2005.

Ferenczi, S. (1928). The adaptation of the family to the child. In: *Final contributions* (pp. 61–76). London: Karnac, 1955.

Ferenczi, S. (1929). The unwelcome child and his death instinct. In: *Final contributions* (pp. 102–107). London: Karnac, 1955.

Ferenczi, S. (1930–32). Notes and fragments. In: *Final contributions* (pp. 216–279). London: Karnac, 1955.1955. [Including Ferenczi, 1931b, 1932b, 1932c.]

Ferenczi, S. (1931a). Child-analysis in the analysis of adults. In: *Final contributions* (pp. 126–142). London: Karnac, 1955.

Ferenczi, S. (1931b). Trauma and anxiety. In: *Final contributions* (pp. 249–250). London: Karnac, 1955.

Ferenczi, S. (1932a). Confusion of tongues between adults and the child. In: *Final contributions* (pp. 156–167). London: Karnac, 1955.

Ferenczi, S. (1932b). On shock [*Uber Erschütterung*]. In: *Final contributions* (pp. 253–254). London: Karnac, 1955.

Ferenczi, S. (1932c). On the revision of the interpretation of dreams [*Zur Revision der Traumdeutung*]. In: *Final contributions* (pp. 240). London: Karnac, 1955.

Ferenczi, S. (1940). *Bausteine zur Psychoanalyse. IV. Band: Gedenkartikel, Kritiken und Referate, Fragmente.* Berne: Hans Huber.

Ferenczi, S. (1955). *Final contributions to the problems and methods of psycho-analysis*, Balint M. (Ed.), Mosbacher et al. (translator). London: Hogarth.

Ferenczi, S. & Groddeck, G. (2002). *The Sándor Ferenczi – Georg Groddeck correspondence 1921–1933.* Fortune C., editor. London: Open Gate Press.

Ferenczi, S. & Rank, O. (1924). *The development of psychoanalysis.* Newton C., translator. Madison, CT: International UP, 1986.

Fergusson, A. (2015). *Cartas imaginarias a Freud y otros ensayos [Imaginary letters to Freud and other essays].* Bogotá, Colombia: Editorial Universidad del Rosario.

Fergusson, A. (2015). *Accompanied Selfrehabilitation.* Bogotá, Colombia: Editorial Universidad del Rosario.

Freud, S. (1896). Further remarks on the neuro-psychoses of defence. *SE 3*, 157–185.

Freud, S. (1905). Three essays on the theory of sexuality. *SE 7*, 123–246.

Freud, S. (1914). On the history of the psycho-analytic movement. *SE 14*, 1–66.

Freud, S. (1918). From the history of an infantile neurosis ('Wolf Man'). *SE 17*, 1–124.

Freud, S. (1920). Beyond the pleasure principle. *SE 18*, 1–64.

Freud, S. (1923). The ego and the id. *SE 19*, 1–66.

Jiménez Avello, J. with Genovés A.) (1998). *Para leer a Ferenczi [To read Ferenczi]*. Madrid: Biblioteca Nueva.

Gallardo, J.V. (1996). *Biografía de Sándor Ferenczi [Biography of Sándor Ferenczi]*. Indepsi.

Gay, P. (1988 ). *Freud: A life for our time.*New York: Norton.

Granoff, W. (2004). *Lacan, Ferenczi y Freud. [Lacan, Ferenczi and Freud]*. Buenos Aires: École lacanienne de psychanalyse.

Grosskurth, P. (1986). *Melanie Klein: Her world and her work*. Harvard University Press.

Gutiérrez-Peláez, M. (2008). The Ferenczian notion of "Orpha" [La noción ferencziana de "Orpha. *Revista Psicoanálisis*, *30*(2–3), 285–290

Gutiérrez-Peláez, M. (2009). Trauma theory in Sándor Ferenczi's writings of 1931 and 1932. *International Journal of Psychoanalysis*, *90*, 1217–1233

Gutiérrez-Peláez, M. (2013). Sándor Ferenczi y la intelectualidad húngara del siglo XX [Sándor Ferenczi and the Hungarian Intelligentsia o the 20th Century]. *Affectio Societatis*, *10*(18), 247–267.

Gutiérrez-Peláez, M. (2015). Ferenczi's anticipation of the traumatic dimension of language: A meeting with Lacan. *Contemporary Psychoanalysis*, *51*(1), 137–154. doi: 10.1080/00107530.2015.957255

Gutiérrez-Peláez, M. (2018). *Confusion of tongues. A Return to Sándo Ferenczi*. London, UK: Routledge.

Gutiérrez-Peláez, M. (2021). Not knowing and not wanting to know Reflections regarding psychosocial and psychotherapeutic intervention in armed conflict scenarios. *Psychoanalytic Psychology*, *38*(4), 348–351 http://dx.doi.org.ez.urosario.edu.co/

Gutiérrez-Peláez, M. & Herrera-Pardo, E. (2017). Environment, trauma and technical innovations: Three links between Donald W. Winnicot and Sándor Ferenczi. *Revista Colombiana de Psiquiatría*, *46*(2), 121–126 doi: 10.1016/j.rcp.2015.12.001

Jacoby, R. (1983). *The repression of psychoanalysis: Otto Fenichel and th political Freudians*. New York, NY: Basic Books.

Jimenez-Avello, J. (2018). The Analytical Technique and the Pathology o Dissociation. 13th International Sándor Ferenczi Conference Florence. May 3–6.

Lacan, J. (1958/2002). The direction of the treatment and the principle of its power. *Écrits. The First Complete Edition in English*. Bruce Fink translator. New York: W. W. Norton and Company.

Lacan, J. (1964/1998). *The four fundamental concepts of psycho-analysis*. Jacques-Alain Miller, Ed.; Alan Sheridan, trans. London: W.W Norton.

Lohser B. & Newton, P.M. (1996). *Unorthodox Freud. The View from the Couch.* New York: Guilford Press.

Lugrin, Y. (2017). *Ferenczi sur le divan de Freud [Ferenczi on Freud's Couch].* France: Campagne Prem.

Márai, S. (1999). *El último encuentro.* Spain: Salamandra.

Masson, J.M. (1984). *The assault on truth: Freud's suppression of the seduction theory.* London: Faber & Faber.

Mészáros, J. (2009). Sándor Ferenczi and the Budapest School of Psychoanalysis. *Psychoanalytic Perspectives, 7*(1), 69–89.

Muñoz de la Cruz, M.L. (1998). El 'diario clínico'. Interdependencia entre la clínica y la técnica psicoanalítica. Acuerdos y diferencias [The 'clinical diary': Interdependence of clinical work and technique in psychoanalysis. Points of agreement and differences]. *Revista Psicoanalítica de la Asociación Psicoanalítica de Madrid, 28,* 9–14.

Newman, G. (2020). "Confusion of tongues". Language, trauma, and transformation in Ingeborg Bachmann's "Simultan". *Journal of Austrian Studies, 53*(2), 1–24.

Rabeyron, T. & Evrard, R. (2012). Historical and contemporary perspectives on occultism in the Freud-Ferenczi correspondence. *Recherches en psychanalyse, 1*(1), 98–111. 10.3917/rep.013.0098

Rachman, A.W. (1997). The suppression and censorship of Ferenczi's confusion of tongues paper. *Psychaoanalytic Inquiry, 17,* 459–485.

Roudinesco, E., & Plon, M. (1997). *Dictionnaire de la psychanalyse.* Paris: Fayard.

Rudnytsky, P. L., Bokay, A., & Giampieri-Deutsch P. (Eds.) (1996). *Ferenczi's turn in psychoanalysis,* NYU Press.

Sabourin, P. (1984). Prefacio. Visir secreto y cabeza de turco [Foreword. Secret vizier and Turk's head]. In: *Ferenczi S. Diario clínico [Clinical Diary]* (pp. 11–20). Buenos Aires: Amorrortu.

Stanton, M., (1997) *Sándor Ferenczi. Reconsiderando la intervención activa [Sándor Ferenczi. Reconsidering the Active Technique];* Tr Juan Gallardo C., Ed.; Andrea Morgado G., Santiago: Bio-Psique.

Strachey, J. (1964). The standard edition of the complete psychological works of Sigmund Freud, Volume XXII (1932–1936): *New Introductory Lectures on Psycho-Analysis and Other Works,* 1–267. London: The Hogarth Press and the Institute of Psycho-analysis.

Sylwan, B. (1984). An untoward event: Ou la guerre du trauma de Breuer a Freud de Jones a Ferenczi.Cahiers Confrontation, *2,* 110–115.

Szokolszky, A. (2016). Hungarian psychology in context. Reclaiming the past. *Hungarian Studies, 30*(1), 17–56.

# Index

Page numbers followed by "n" indicate a note

Abraham, Karl 27, 54
accompanied auto analysis 7
Accompanied Self-rehabilitation (ASR) 114
active therapy 47
adult–child relationship 81
aggression 88
Aguirre, Francisco Javier 102
Alexander, Franz 30, 108
analytical transference 95
antipathy 92
anxiety 78, 82
Aron, Lewis 110
atomisation 83
autonomous personality 110
autotomy 87–8

Bakhtin, Mikhail 115
Bak, Róbert 30
Balint, Michael 5, 19, 60, 102, 108
Barthodeiszky 22
Bártok, Béla 12
Benedek, Teréz 30
Bentham, Jeremy 115
Berény, Róbert 12
bio-analysis 57
body-mind dualism 86
Borgogno 110

Bresler, Johannes 18

Cabré, M. 93
Castillo, Beatriz 101
castration 36
Center for Psychosocial Studies (CEPSS) 3
child analysis 35
child's babbling 45
*Clinical Diary* 4, 11, 23, 43, 44, 57, 60, 77, 81, 89–99
clinical difficulty 61
clinical innovation 109
counter-transference 80n1, 91

dementia 21
depressive anxiety 36
deprivation 70
development of character 81
dialogue of unconsciouses 92
Dupont, Judith 76, 81, 101

ego 43, 59
emotional functioning 99
emotional needs 92, 93, 95
emotional reaction 89
Etcheverri, José Luis 102
Evans, D. 46

external aggressor 83

female masochism 86
female passivity 86
Ferenczi, Sándor: active therapy,
    development in 47; adult
    hypocrisy, criticism 68; approach
    to paranoia 17; The Budapest
    school of psychoanalysis 107–9;
    clinical and theoretical work 2;
    clinical difficulty 61; clinical
    innovations 91; clinical
    interventions 97; for clinical
    practice 9; concept of
    introjection 38; concept of "scar
    formation" 75; cross-fertilization
    of psychoanalysis 28;
    democratisation of
    psychoanalysis 7; deprivation 70;
    development of sexuality 57;
    devoted to social change 2, 12;
    education, affirm of 38; erratic
    writing style 23; fragmentation
    of mental life 75; with Freud's
    work 16–9, 48–52; geological
    vicissitudes, influence of 22; and
    Gizella Pálos relations 24–6;
    with Groddeck relations 52–3;
    hypnagogic hallucinations 51;
    hypnosis relations 36; idea of
    original monism 34; infantile
    sexual desires 38–6; innovation
    and creativity 8; interest on
    psychoanalysis 16; interests in
    telepathy 19; lectures and
    influence in Spain 73–80; mutual
    relaxation 92; patient's split
    personality 61; privation 70;
    process of resurrection 6; psychic
    mechanism of melancholy 20;
    psychological differences in
    children 70; psychological
    functioning 98; sexual abuses
    and excesses 11; sexual
    intercourse, approach problem
    of 20; social and cultural
    influence 28; social and political
    transformation 2; social
    commitment and political
    convictions 23; somatic
    symptoms 21; teachers and
    parent relations 66; technical
    innovations 43, 46; theory of
    trauma 81–6; transference 32, 35;
    translation work 24;
    traumatogenesis, research on 75;
    work on other languages 101; in
    writing poetry 11
Fergusson, Alberto 3, 99n1, 114
fragmentation 83
France, Anatole 19
Fränkel, Bernath 9
Freud, Anna 35, 47, 54, 82
Freud, Martin 78
Freud, Sigmund: conception of
    death drive 58; concept of
    countertransference 99; early
    stages of psychoanalysis 6;
    emotional and practical aspects
    55; hypnosis 37, 38; ideas on
    transference 35; initial ego/
    reality 34; intrapsychic
    transference and clinical
    transference 32; phylogenetic
    approaches 21; protophantasies
    36; psychoanalytic community
    81; purified-pleasure-ego 34;
    with Sándor Ferenczi's work
    16–9, 48–52; seduction theory
    76; self-analysis 24; traumatic
    theory 83
frustration, principle of 42

Gadamer, Hans-Georg 115
Genovés, Agustín 31–3
Granoff, Wladimir 60
Groddeck, George 52–3, 110
Gutiérrez-Peláez, Miguel 3,
    110, 115

Haeckel, E. H. A. 57
Hárnik, Jenõ 30
Harris, Adrienne 110
Hauser, Arnold 12
Heidegger, Martin 115
Heilprin, Michael 9
Hirschfeld, Magnus 15
Hollós, István 27
homosexuals/homosexuality 15, 22
humanity 21
Hungarian Psychoanalytic
    Society 73
hypnagogic hallucinations 51
hypnosis 36, 38, 54
hypochondria 50
hysteria 32

infantile sexual desires 38, 39
International Psychoanalytic
    Association (IPA) 8
*Interpretation of dreams* 31
intersubjective psychoanalysis 110
intoxication and withdrawal
    syndrome 22
introjection, concept of 38

Jacoby, Russell 7
Jászi, Oszkár 12
Johnson, Alvin Saunders 109
Jones, Ernest 49
Jung, Gustav 12, 40

Karinthy, Frédéric 66
Karinthy, Frigyes 12, 94
Kleinian theory 35
Klein, Melanie 30, 35, 54, 56, 69,
    106, 108
Kosztolányi, Dezsõ 12

Lacan, Jacques 38, 43–5, 60
Levi, Lajos 78
libidinal frustration 42
Lóránd, Sándor 30
Losher, Beate 6

love: adult's erotic current 82;
    child's tender love 82
Lukács, György 12, 29

Mahler, Margaret 108
manic emotion 22
Mannheim, Karl 12
Márai, Sándor 12, 104
Marx, Karl 4, 115
masturbation 69
melancholic suicide 20
melancholy 22
mental health issues 113
mental illnesses 113
Meyer, Adolf 56
Mitchell, Stephen A. 110
Möbius, Paul Julius 15
mutual analysis 7, 43, 91, 95–6, 97
mutual relaxation 92

neurosis 65
neurotic mendacity 62
neutrality 16
Newton, Peter M. 6

object-hate 35
object-love 35
obsessional intellectuality 64
obsessive neuroses 32
obsessive neurosis 21
omnipotence 38
"Orpha," concept of 94

Pankejeff, Sergei 63
paranoid dementia 22
passionate punishments 37
pathoneuroses 50
Peirce, Charles Sanders 115
persecutory anxiety 36
personality 80n1, 82
pre-Freudian therapies 18
primordial transferences 35
privation 70
psychic reality 62

psychoanalysis: cross-fertilization of 28; democratisation of 7; disseminated psychoanalysis 28; liberal socialism 13; political possibilities of 13; revolution of 6; self-salvation of individual 13; in social sphere 12; subversive and marginal character of 104; therapeutic potential of 74
psychoanalytic community 81
psychoanalytic discoveries 113
psychoanalytic discretion 96
psychoanalytic doctrine 14
psychoanalytic movement 15, 30, 73; in Hungary 27, 29; internal disputes of 49
psychoanalytic societies 4
psychoanalytic technique 61
psychoanalytic training 65
psychological needs 95
psychology, development of 9
psychoneurosis 82
psychosocial interventions 115
psychosomatics 52
psychotic manifestations 101

Radó, Sándor 30, 108
Rank, Otto 49
Rapaport, David 30, 108
regression 45
relational psychoanalysis 109, 110
Róheim, Géza 12, 30

sadistic sexual intercourse 36
Safran, Jeremy 110
Salomé, Lou Andreas 115
Sándor Ferenczi Center 109–11
scar formation, concept of 75
seduction 36, 76
self-abandonment 87
self, neoformation of 89
Severn, Elizabeth 4
sexual intrusion 82
sleep 45

social change 12
sociology 6
Sokolnicka, Eugénie 50, 51
somatic psychology 21
split personality 61
Stanton, M. 27, 110
state of confusion 89
Stein, Füllöp 16
Sullivan, H.S 56
super-ego 36, 69
sympathy 92
Szilard, Leo 107

technical innovations 43, 46, 93
Teller, Edward 107
temporary illusion 67
The interpretation of dreams (1900) 12
theory of psychosomatics 21
Thompson, Clara 77
Tószeghi, Antal Freund 12
transference neuroses 31
transference of unconscious 32
trauma 81–6; confusion of tongues 84; external aggressor 83; memory and remembering 84; psychic shock 85
traumata 68
traumatic fixation 90

uncertainties 110
unconscious 43, 64, 65, 66, 73; functioning 99; mental forces 37
Unorthodox Freud 6

Varga, Jenő 29, 30
Viennese Psychoanalysis 6
von Krafft-Ebing, Richard 15

Watson, John B. 56
Winnicott, Donald W. 69, 110

Zeltner, Ernö 105